PLAYS FOR ENGLAND

WATCH IT COME DOWN

John Osborne

PLAYS FOR ENGLAND

THE BLOOD OF THE BAMBERGS
UNDER PLAIN COVER

WATCH IT COME DOWN

OBERON BOOKS
LONDON

Contents

INTRODUCTION

Charles Wood

I never saw the two plays comprising *Plays for England* when they were first produced at the Royal Court in 1962, but I wish I had, and when you read *The Blood of the Bambergs* and *Under Plain Cover* I'm sure you'll feel the same. They are however, said to be the first time that the Royal Court lost money on John Osborne. "(His) magnetic name failed to overcome the English playgoer's resistance to double bills" (Irving Wardle, *The Theatres of George Devine*, 1978).

John Osborne describes *The Blood of the Bambergs* as a fairy tale, and says in the second volume of his autobiography (John Osborne, *A Better Class of Person*, 1991) that it is "simply a broadly satiric account of one of the permanent fixtures of English life, a Royal Wedding" and that "It seems a good idea to match the shuffling pantomime of contemporary royal fantasy with the real, romantic thing."

The Blood of the Bambergs

The Bambergs are a royal family, very like the Windsors but still very Germanic. They have obviously had no reason to change their names – which removes the First World War, when they might just have been mistaken for the other side, from their history – and Prince Will in this play is a Wilhelm not a William. Sadly, for he appears to be a perfect prince for England, ruthless and a simpleton, he dies on the way to his wedding – driving his fast sports car along a motorway specially cleared of all obstacles, the only way he can usually be trusted to arrive anywhere in one piece. This time the system has failed him, he has hit a concrete road block put in place for his protection from lesser drivers, and Princess Melanie is in danger of being left at the altar.

With a little help from Anthony Hope – someone John Osborne was happy to plagiarise for he, like many of us, loved paddling in the pools of Ruritania – two killings and an Australian cameraman who discovers he has Bamberg blood (if somewhat diluted by its washing in the womb of a "pretty little thing, blonde, very blonde... She was the only blonde he ever had") a solution is found. All the cameraman needs to do is shave off his beard, let his large Bamberg ears flap loose, his huge Bamberg nose find its newly elevated level and the throne of England is safe.

Princess Melanie doesn't mind much for it seems she is bored. It is boring being a royal, very very boring: "you'll crumble and disintegrate with boredom. Your blood will rush with constant hot and cold running boredom." Our cameraman is undeterred, he's after the loot, and there's enough Bamberg blood left in him to make sure that he'll see very little beyond the length of his quite long nose even when Princess Melanie chillingly cries: "Oh, my God, I am so bored... and most of all, I am bored with you, my people, my loyal subjects, I am so bored that even this cheap little Australian looks like relieving it for a few, brief moments, now and then, in the rest of my lifetime."

When first produced *The Blood of the Bambergs* must have seemed to owe more to *The Prisoner of Zenda* than the spectacularly dull home life of our own dear Royals, and note that in 1962 it was still expected that royals would embrace the Ruritanian notion of marriage for the rest of life.

Now, in 1999, several royal weddings, divorces, catastrophic indiscretions, extraordinarily bad choices of mate or lover, numerous incidences of bull-headed Bamberg-like insensitivity and stupidity later, we must surely view our own Royals in a very different light and thank God that they have broken loose, thrown down the gauntlet of their insecurity before us, shown us their despair and their incompetence, put themselves well beyond being entrusted with real power ever again; become the Republicans I'm sure they have always secretly longed to be.

Which leaves us with Lt-Colonel Taft and his ilk. In the play Taft is a loyal servant and a murderous much-decorated thug who looks on the royal family as "A whole way of life. We are its servants, instruments of order, decency and all the things that have made life honourable and tolerable for a thousand years." He and his like are not going to be happy with their collapsed world.

It isn't the poor sad inconsequential royals we have to fear – they only really want to be left alone to their comforting charades, infidelities and adulteries like the rest of us; it's the cloak-spreaders looking for the puddles of advancement, and the self-righteous assassins, who use the promise of honour as ruthlessly as a pistol to destroy creative subversion.

John Osborne was never offered an honour of any kind but I'm certain he would have accepted one; after all, to laugh and say yes is the perfect antidote to such poisonous temptings.

(Incidentally, when looking up just how many royal weddings there had been between the Second World War and 1962 I came across a curious honour granted to Princess Margaret. She is, believe it or not, "the only member of the present Royal Family other than Queen Elizabeth The Queen Mother to hold the Royal Victorian Chain" (*The Royal Encyclopaedia*). I wonder who did it for her before?)

Under Plain Cover

In 1737 the Stage Licensing Act was passed, and from that date all plays had to be read by the Lord Chamberlain's Office before being given a licence.

John Osborne, like most English playwrights before 1968, was very familiar with the walk up St James's to the Palace for an ex-Grenadier Lt-Colonel's expert "You can't pull the wool over my eyes laddie!" view, on such monumentally important issues as the amount of "rodgering" and talk of "rodgering" to be allowed before being granted a licence to perform. With a little planning we might all have met like tour actors on a railway station platform in Crewe on Sunday, to swap and hone our euphemisms.

He was mildly relieved that the Lord Chamberlain's Office had found nothing to complain of in *Under Plain Cover* but George Devine, the Artistic Director of the English Stage Company at the Royal Court, was "bemused by St James's Palace's lack of response to the repetition of 'knickers' some forty-five times in less than an hour" (John Osborne, *A Better Class of Person*).

In *Under Plain Cover*, Tim and Jenny play their games and rehearse their own private neuroses in a manner at first amusing and then achingly sad. The repetition of the word "knickers" reaches a stage where you long for it not to be said, because with every repetition it becomes more revealing. Then their secret is out. They are not the happily married young couple with two children they seem to be. The tabloids are on to them, their "human interest story" is splashed across the front page and they are driven apart. The respectability of public confession and redemption through embracing the mundane is thrust upon them by a reporter looking for a sensational front-page photo to satisfy his editor.

Their story is the stuff of high romance, the real stuff, and the real devotion beneath the paraphernalia of ambition and convention and role playing that is progress through life. John Russell Taylor saw it as the fourth act of *Look Back in Anger*; "what could have happened to Jimmy and Alison a few years after they were reunited."

Watch it Come Down

A few years ago I stood at the two-weeks-old grave of John Osborne with another playwright of my long acquaintance and he asked me if I thought the plays "would live". It seemed to me to be an impertinent question and I still think so for if any proof is needed of the timelessness of John Osborne's plays, a reading of *Watch it Come Down* should suffice. I saw the play when it was first produced at the National Theatre in 1976 and remember particularly the touching performance of Michael Gough as Glen, who waits in the old parcels office of a one-time railway station for death, while his friends scar and trash each other and themselves in the real waiting rooms. It is he who provides the forlorn title: "It said 'Blenkinsop – Demolitionists. We *do* it. You *watch* it. *Come down.*'"

Charles Wood
London 1999

THE BLOOD OF
THE BAMBERGS

a fairy story

Characters

WIMPLE

LEMON

BROWN

TAFT

WITHERS

RUSSELL

FOOTMAN

WOMAN

MELANIE

THE BAMBERGS

FIVE JOURNALISTS

ARCHBISHOP

The Blood of the Bambergs was first performed at the Royal Court Theatre, London, on 19 July 1962, by the English Stage Company. It was directed by John Dexter and the film sequence was by John Dexter, Desmond Davies and Tony Gibbs. The décor was by Alan Tagg. The cast was as follows:

WIMPLE, James Cossins

CAMERAMAN, John Maynard

LEMON, Billy Russell

FLOOR ASSISTANT, Barbara Keogh

BROWN, Glyn Owen

TAFT, Graham Crowden

WITHERS, Anton Rodgers

GUARDS, Tony Caunter, Jimmy Gardner

RUSSELL, John Meillon

1ST FOOTMAN, Charles Lewsen

2ND FOOTMAN, Norman Allen

3RD FOOTMAN, John Maynard

WOMAN, Avril Elgar

MELANIE, Vivian Pickles

ARCHBISHOP, Alan Bennett

1ST JOURNALIST, Robin Chapman

2ND JOURNALIST, Barbara Keogh

3RD JOURNALIST, Tony Caunter

4TH JOURNALIST, Constance Lorne

5TH JOURNALIST, Jimmy Gardner

Act One: Late one night in the Cathedral
Act Two: Scene 1: A room in the Palace early next morning
Scene 2: The Cathedral later that day

ACT ONE

Before the altar of a large Gothic cathedral. In the wispy yellow light of an empty cathedral, a boyish-looking, portly man of middle age is staring up around him in well-groomed humility. As a few hollow hammering sounds die away he turns to the audience, coughs discreetly into his sleeve and speaks in an easy, sober and confidential voice. Around his neck, nestled against his ample silk shirt, is a small microphone. In his hand he is carrying a larger one. His name is PAUL WIMPLE. In a corner, seated and leaning against some scaffolding is a casually dressed, bearded young man about thirty. Around his neck hangs a Rolleiflex, and he is lighting himself a cigarette. He looks bored and exhausted.

WIMPLE: Those sounds you heard just then
    echoing far, far above my head here and dying
    away in the secret corners of this great cathedral
    were probably the last sounds we shall hear from
    this place tonight.
    *(There is a reverberating clanging of tubular steel on stone
    and a muffled shout.)*
    Oh no, I was wrong, someone else is still here.
    That sound you heard was the strange muffled
    noise of men working, working into the night,
    whilst most of the country lies –
    (Another clang and more hollow shouts.)
    – lies sleeping, quietly, patiently and with love
    – I think I may say, quite unselfconsciously,
    with love. They have been labouring into the
    night in preparation for the tremendous events
    of the morrow. For what they are doing is,
    indeed, a labour of great love, as great as that
    which impelled those men seven centuries ago
    when they applied their ancient skills and crafts
    to the building of this great cathedral for the
    remembrance of man and to the glory of God.
    For in a few hours' time – twelve and a half to
    be exact – and on this very spot, the moment

which millions of people throughout the world
have awaited with such expectation will arrive
and two very famous people will be united in
holy matrimony; and united amid all the pomp
and splendour that a proud and grateful nation
can provide on such occasions for her most
illustrious ones. On this very spot where I am
standing now – no, a little more to my left
I think, if I am not mistaken. Anyway, I shall be
talking to the Archbishop himself in a few
moments and I have no doubt he will very soon
put me right. But as I say, on this very spot
where I am standing now, in the tremendous,
rather severe perhaps, but tremendous hush of
this great cathedral where kings and queens and
noble princes are interred, where there is no man
honoured who was ever mean – as a great poet
once put it – in this place tomorrow, at a little
past one o'clock we shall be privileged to watch
the most solemn occasion in our national life –
a royal wedding. Yes, Princess Melanie is to
marry Prince Wilhelm or, as I think we might
venture to call him, as they all seem to do, at
least in this part of the country, our Prince Will.
Our Prince Will will – Wilhelm will – be the
first royal bridegroom to have walked down this
magnificent nave for over a year and what
a thrill it is when we remember those many
happy – and solemn – but happy occasions. It is
well perhaps to remember them, for as I say,
looking around me now, into the lofty recesses of
this soaring, gaunt and ancient house of worship,
it is difficult to believe that shortly this still,
silent place will be the very centre of such
glorious splendour, such colour and trappings,
such grandeur and, yes, I think I must say again,
such solemnity. The last arrangements have been
made, the vast technical complications have

been tied up. Television cameras have been hoisted into their resting places, the last workman has put away his tools and all that is left is silence – silence, that is, except for my voice. There is something strangely unreal about it all. Silence and space, but in that very space is something living, tho' it be silent. Perhaps it is even possible to hear it. If you listen carefully. If there is a place anywhere at all tonight where it might be said that this nation's heart beats it must surely be here – where I am standing now – but before we finally take our leave tonight, I should like you to meet some of the people who have been responsible for the arrangements of the morrow. Months of intricate planning go into these arrangements and tonight we have here just one or two of these people who have dedicated themselves to this task. (*LEMON enters.*)

They range from, shall I say, the humblest – no, not the humblest, for his job is an extremely skilled one, no – rather from the proudest of living craftsmen to some of the highest in the land. First, I have with me here Mr Charlie Lemon. Mr Lemon is the foreman in charge of all the workmen, the workmen whose – work – we have heard going on or, rather, coming to a close. Mr Lemon, it must be a relief to you to know that your part in all this is virtually over?

LEMON: Well yes, I shall be quite glad to get home and put my feet up, quite frankly.

WIMPLE: But you must feel a tremendous sense of achievement to have finished everything in time?

LEMON: Oh yes, I do.

WIMPLE: What exactly is it you have been doing?

LEMON: Well, mainly seeing to all the seating facilities, etcetera, and supervising the erection of spectators' stands outside the cathedral itself as well as many of the more important stands all the way along the route.

WIMPLE: I see, well that's certainly what you would call a very responsible job indeed.

LEMON: Yes, well, it is really, I suppose.

WIMPLE: Very responsible indeed. Tell me, Mr Lemon –

LEMON: Yes?

WIMPLE: How long have you been engaged in these preparations?

LEMON: Oh, months.

WIMPLE: Months, really?

LEMON: Oh yes, months and months.

WIMPLE: And how many men are involved in this work?

LEMON: I have under me at the present time nine hundred and forty-seven, that's if my memory serves me right.

WIMPLE: Nearly a thousand men and what are they?

LEMON: What do you mean, what are they?

WIMPLE: I mean what do they do?

LEMON: Oh, there are builders, carpenters, electricians, plumbers and all sorts.

WIMPLE: Craftsmen of every kind in fact, and all working at top speed for months.

LEMON: Years, really.

WIMPLE: Years?

LEMON: Most of the men engaged in this type of work are employed on what is in fact a more or less permanent basis, although there was a falling off a year or so ago after the Coronation, but then it picked up again recently. Of course, as you know we've had two funerals and one christening; that is a lesser occasion for us, of course, on this side anyhow, but they are still much more elaborate than they were a few years ago.

WIMPLE: (*Brings LEMON farther down stage.*) So
　　you have been yourself a specialist in this work
　　for quite some considerable time?

LEMON: Yes, you could say that. I suppose about
　　seventeen years on and off. On mostly.

WIMPLE: That must be an almost unique record.

LEMON: No, no, I wouldn't say that. There are lots
　　of chaps, dozens I should say, who were in it
　　with me from the beginning, you might say.

WIMPLE: The beginning?

LEMON: Yes, from the beginning, the earliest
　　beginnings of the industry, from the time that it
　　ceased to simply be an ancient craft and became
　　the thriving, modern industry that it is today. You
　　see, when I started, it was never much more than
　　a part-time job, practically all casual labour.

WIMPLE: And do you think, then, that conditions
　　have changed a great deal?

LEMON: Oh yes most definitely and emphatically.

WIMPLE: In what particular way, would you say?

LEMON: Principally in the – in the – in the –

WIMPLE: In the status of the individual workman,
　　I imagine.

LEMON: That's right, the status of the
　　individual workman.

WIMPLE: In the pride, in fact, of being
　　employed in such a vital, thriving and forward-
　　looking industry?

LEMON: Yes, I should say that, yes.

WIMPLE: And would you, for instance, recommend
　　a young man about to start his working life to
　　enter this industry? For example, would you,
　　encourage your own son to go into it?

LEMON: I would, most definitely; as a matter of
　　fact it was my son who laid the carpet you've
　　been standing on.

WIMPLE: Well, I must be careful where I put my
　　muddy boots then.

LEMON: Yes, my son is now chief assistant in
   charge of all carpet-laying arrangements.
WIMPLE: You must be a very proud man, Mr Lemon.
LEMON: Oh yes, definitely. He has always been
   a good boy.
WIMPLE: I wish you could see this carpet, ladies
   and gentlemen, in the flesh as it were, beautifully
   laid with infinite love and skill.
LEMON: Always been good to his mother.
WIMPLE: (*Crosses to LEMON.*) I'm sure. And there
   is really nothing else you would rather have
   done in life?
LEMON: Nothing.
WIMPLE: Nothing at all?
LEMON: No, I think I can say that quite honestly
   and sincerely. Of course, I am only responsible
   for one small section of the industry, but I think
   I can honestly say, in all sincerity, that in all
   the time in which I have been associated with it
   I have never been tempted to do anything else.
WIMPLE: One last question, Mr Lemon.
LEMON: And what would that be?
WIMPLE: Is it true that the working hours in your
   industry are far longer than the national average?
LEMON: That is true, Mr Wimple. That is true.
   But you must remember this. There is a very
   special benefit which – comes out of simply –
   the privilege of being a worker – in this industry.
WIMPLE: Yes.
LEMON: That is to say, Mr Wimple, a man who
   has a special pride in his job, a man who knows
   that what he is doing makes a difference to the
   world he's living in, who knows he's making
   a vital contribution to the greatness of this
   country. That man is a happy man, Mr Wimple,
   and a contented worker, and for why? I'll tell you
   for why. Because he is a fulfilled man, and how
   many people in these troubled times can say that
   today?

WIMPLE: (*Down to LEMON, crosses to his left to take him off.*) All too few, Mr Lemon, thank you.

LEMON: (*Warming up.*) I myself, just in my section mind you, I have calculated that during the past seventeen years in which I have had the honour to do this job, I could have built, using the same materials and labour, you understand, 27 secondary modern schools and 1,200,000 houses.

WIMPLE: (*Pulls LEMON off.*) Thank you, Mr Lemon.

LEMON: Thank *you*, Mr Wimple.

WIMPLE: Now, as I told you earlier, I am to have the privilege of talking with His Grace the Archbishop himself. In fact, it was first arranged that we should have a filmed interview earlier today so that it wouldn't be necessary to impose too great a strain on him just before – the momentous events of the – morrow, in which, of course, he is, what you might call the leading actor. Apart from the principals that is. Naturally. (*ASSISTANT enters left of WIMPLE. Hands him a note.*) However, His Grace was unable to come and talk to me as we had arranged, owing to his overlapping commitments in which, of course, his religious, that is to say his formal religious activities must inevitably play a part. Well now, someone has just handed me a note saying that His Grace asks to be excused from our meeting tonight as he is still deeply immersed in the preparations for his own vital role. (*ASSISTANT goes out.*) You might think that by this time such a thing would hold little terror for an old, experienced hand at the game but this, of course, is to *ignore,* or at least to devalue, the overwhelming spiritual burden involved. As any actor will tell you, the three-hundredth performance of *Hamlet* may well be the most trying and taxing of all. A familiarity may breed, not contempt, but despair. I am sure you will join with me in wholeheartedly wishing His Grace good luck for yet another first night. (*WIMPLE moves down stage.*) It is now – er – by my watch, eight minutes past twelve and according to our report here the Prince is at this moment speeding along in his car to be in good time at his appointed place tomorrow. As he drives along, like any other young man in his powerful sports car – and the Prince is a very fine, skilful and fast driver, as I have reason to know, I have watched him on several occasions – as he drives along, I wonder what his thoughts are. Well, that we shall never know of course, but although he will need to keep his mind on the road, just like any other young man – he will, no doubt, *be* thinking – but that will be made a little easier at any rate as the Ministry concerned has cleared the entire length of the highway for 24 hours for the exclusive use of the Prince, the Royal Party and, of course, other guests. The man responsible for this operation is, as you may know, Mr Ted Brown, the newly appointed Minister of Culture. We have been able to persuade Mr Brown to talk to us for a few minutes on the eve of what is, you might say, his first big production. (*Brings BROWN from left. Assembly to left centre.*) He is here with me now so I won't waste his time but ask you right away, Mr Brown: you'd really call this your first big assignment would you not?

BROWN: That is substantially correct. My Ministry as you know was only created by the Prime Minister a few months ago, shortly after the General Election.

WIMPLE: I suppose it would be true to say that the United Socialist Party more or less fought the Election on this very issue, on the creation of your Ministry.

BROWN: We did. Naturally I would not wish to indulge in anything like party politics on the eve of a joyous and – solemn – occasion like this, but it is certainly true to say that my Ministry and its function in preparing this occasion and all the others like it, is a direct result of a deliberate political programme. The policy was *hammered* out in our usual democratic way, the dissident minority was expelled and the resultant united effort –

WIMPLE: Yes, well –

BROWN: United –

WIMPLE: The thing I want to –

BROWN: United Socialist effort, I must add –

WIMPLE: Yes, as you say, these petty squabbles of political life –

BROWN: Ah yes – I think it must be said all the same.

WIMPLE: Up until a few months ago, this great industry was under the direct control of a few individuals appointed by the King personally and whose offices were hallowed by time and tradition. Mr Brown, do you think that by making a Government department directly responsible, it will really lead to an improvement in what has always been, up to now, a superb public service?

BROWN: Well, of course, that is a question we have been hearing a great deal about, and there is no doubt that it is one that has dominated the public interest and will probably go on doing so for some considerable time. Quite naturally, I am particularly aware of it as I am personally, not only the centre of the controversy, but I think I can say, without taking any credit away from the Prime Minister and my colleagues, I have been from the first, one of the architects of the whole policy.

WIMPLE: But do you think it will lead to an improvement? I mean, how will the creation of your Ministry affect the ordinary man in the street?

BROWN: Well, I should be able to answer that question, *but I have to say*, and I think it is not an immodest claim in the circumstances, that the reason I was chosen for this major post in the Cabinet – is that I am – well, the man in the street. I know him, he knows me. I know what he feels and I try to make damn sure he knows what I feel. (*ASSISTANT enters from right. Assembly to left of WIMPLE. Hands him a note.*) Which is what I am going to try to accomplish now, Mr Wimple, so that you can get on with your programme and I can get on with my job. As you said yourself, it is difficult to discuss this whole question without reference to party politics, but I will do my best.

WIMPLE: Your post was hitherto held by the Guardian of the King's Household, was it not?

BROWN: It was, and very ably indeed, by Lieutenant-Colonel Taft.

WIMPLE: (*Crosses to right of BROWN.*) Colonel Taft was to have been with us by now, Ladies and Gentlemen, but a report came through that he has been delayed somewhere on the – on the – highway. But we have every reason to believe he will be here very shortly, so we may have an opportunity of talking to him. (*To BROWN.*) Would you say that Colonel Taft is still making an important contribution to this solemn occasion?

BROWN: He most certainly is. I must be absolutely frank and tell you that I simply would not have known my way around during those first difficult months at the Ministry without Colonel Taft. His experience, his infinite craftsmanship and his dedicated feeling for the job are unique – absolutely unequalled.

WIMPLE: So that the jobs filled by individuals like Colonel Taft have not become in any way obsolete?

BROWN: Not at all, quite the opposite. We need people like Colonel Taft as much as we ever have and what's more we still need many, many more like him. It is simply a question of changing the machinery. The old, private, simple methods just wouldn't do any more. I am sorry to keep saying it, but I am afraid I have to because a lot of people still go around creating the wrong impression, not only about my Ministry, but about the whole basis of the policy of this Government – simply because they will get hold of the wrong end of the stick.

WIMPLE: Yes.

BROWN: (*Takes microphone from WIMPLE and crosses to down left.*) Listen comrades, let's not beat about the bush. What is the position of this country in the world today? Where do we stand, what is our position, what is our special contribution to the free countries of the West? Wherein lies our strength? Wherein? There is no ignoring the facts any longer: we are hanging to the cliff face of morality and, what's more, we're hanging by our fingernails. This old country that was for so long a leader is, alas, falling behind in the race. As we look around at this land that once gave so richly and lift up our eyes we can only ask: from whence cometh our help? Well, let us face it, who's going to bother with us? The brutal fact is there is not going to be any help, not if we lift up our eyes to the hills or anywhere else. No, the only help we can look to is self-help. Now a lot of people think that by that we mean help yourself. Or, I should say, a few people – a few people who have always just been out for themselves. They only wanted a few people to help themselves. But we believe (*He crosses to the right of WIMPLE.*) that everyone,

25

without exception, should learn to help
themselves. And I am thinking particularly of the
old age pensioners.

WIMPLE: Ah, yes.

BROWN: Who are fast becoming such a strong and
important section of our community. Not only
can we boast of having more old age pensioners
than any other European country, but there can
be no doubt that the time is not too far distant
when they will form at least an electoral majority.

WIMPLE: You have allocated, let me see, twenty-
five per cent of all the seats along the route to
old age pensioners, haven't you?

BROWN: I have.

WIMPLE: There has been a certain amount of
strong criticism of this decision in various
quarters, hasn't there?

BROWN: There has.

WIMPLE: And it has been suggested that in
view of the large number of women, and
particularly children, who get killed in these
mass demonstrations of – loyalty and affection –
it might have been wiser to have given priority
to them.

BROWN: Yes, well of course, I am quite familiar
with that argument.

WIMPLE: But you don't believe it has any validity?

BROWN: I do not. I think it is based on muddled
thinking that is completely at variance with all
our beliefs and way of life. It is, as we all know,
a sad fact that these joyous occasions are always
and inevitably accompanied by a considerable
number of deaths. And I regret to say that these
figures have been steadily rising. They even
exceed the figures for deaths on the road – and
you know how concerned we were about them.
We thought *that* was a problem. However, this is
the market price of progress and of civilisation.

It is inescapable. But, as regards my concession to old age pensioners, this matter has been given considerable attention by His Majesty's Government and I can tell you now, there is no question of our going back on it.

WIMPLE: You don't think that this privilege will cause widespread ill-feeling towards old people?

BROWN: There has always been widespread ill-feeling towards old people. No, I am afraid that just isn't my philosophy. If so many hundreds of people are to be trampled to death, let the old people take their chance too, that is the argument. No, I say – certainly not. I believe that the old must be protected as well as anyone. However, let's not look on the gloomy side. Whatever the figures may or may not be on this particular occasion it's going to be yet another wonderful, heart-warming, magnificent ceremony. I don't deny that there are some dry doctrinaire old sticks around to complain about the gew-gaws. You will always get long-faced old grouchers like that. Why, we used to have enough trouble with them in the old days of my own party before we slung them out. Before the United Socialist Party came into being that is. Puritans, I suppose you'd call them. Anyway, I think we can safely say that they have never represented anyone but themselves and, thank God, there's only a handful left these days anyway.

WIMPLE: So you're not anticipating any active opposition from your old political opponent?

BROWN: I am not. I believe that particular gentleman you are referring to has given up political life altogether. Besides, I doubt whether we shall ever see him again in this country. No, you see, the trouble with such people is that they always misinterpret the Mood of the People.

WIMPLE: Or perhaps they interpret it too well.
(*TAFT enters from left. Assembly, crosses to WIMPLE, followed by WITHERS.*)
Ah, now here is Colonel Taft. Good evening, Colonel.

TAFT: Eh? Withers! (*He crosses to BROWN.*)

WIMPLE: And with him, I think, is his aide, Captain Withers.

WITHERS: Good evening. I am afraid we have – we have – come to take the Minister away from you.

TAFT: (*To BROWN.*) Will you be long, sir?

BROWN: Just a few minutes.

TAFT: Ah.

WIMPLE: (*Crosses to centre.*) You look as if you have had a hard drive, sir.

TAFT: Good. What's that you say?

WIMPLE: We are unaccustomed to seeing *you* look flustered in any way.
(*TAFT and WITHERS move up stage, pace from left to right. BROWN takes mike from WIMPLE, crosses to down left. WIMPLE up on to rostrum, looks at TAFT and WITHERS, turns down.*)

BROWN: In conclusion, comrades, I would just ask you to remember this: our race is not yet run and it is not yet lost. We have time. We have ourselves. There was a time, for instance, when the Roman Mass was a profound experience in which all men were able to participate and which united the Western world. What unites the world today? Nothing. Everywhere there is strife and disagreement but what united *us*? What makes this little proud land one? I will tell you: what we in this country have managed to do is to isolate – to isolate the poetical element in our faith. We have been able to reconstitute our lives. We have based our socialism on a common shared experience. We have found the poetical imperative. I do not have to remind you how we had lost it. But now it is found again and let us rejoice. Good night. Oh, and don't forget, if you are demonstrating tomorrow, don't, I repeat, don't, have that extra drink. If you are going to be loyal, be sober. You may save a life. (*He hands the microphone to WIMPLE.*)

WIMPLE: Thank you, sir. And now that very colourful, dignified and familiar figure, Colonel Taft. Colonel Taft, whom we associate with many, many superb and historical moments in the past, and, who has indeed been largely responsible for them – Colonel Taft.

TAFT: (*Crosses to WIMPLE.*) Eh?

WIMPLE: Many people will probably be anxious to know your feelings tomorrow when you will, for the first time, be taking a back seat, as it were.

TAFT: Back seat? What back seat? I don't know what you're talking about. (*Crosses left of WIMPLE.*)

WITHERS: I'm sorry, Mr Wimple.

WIMPLE: Yes?

WITHERS: I'm afraid it's not possible for Colonel Taft to speak to you just now.

WIMPLE: Yes. Of course. Perhaps you, Captain Withers –

WITHERS: Please excuse me. (*Crosses to BROWN and TAFT.*)

WIMPLE: Well, there we are, ladies and gentlemen, we must bring now our programme to a close. (*Moves down stage left.*) As Colonel Taft and his aide Captain Withers discuss some last-minute details let me remind you that we shall be returning here tomorrow at twelve o'clock noon, that is, and I hope you will be able to join me in witnessing what will surely be yet another – day of joy. Good night.

(*WIMPLE hands his microphone to a technician and with a curious and casual glance at WITHERS he calls out amiably.*) Nothing gone wrong?

WITHERS: Wrong?

WIMPLE: Yes, you looked a bit pale just now.

WITHERS: What could possibly go wrong?

WIMPLE: (*Goes out left.*) Yes, silly question, old boy. Good night.

WITHERS: Good night.

(*Left alone TAFT and WITHERS stare anxiously at BROWN. He looks stricken. WITHERS, BROWN and TAFT move to front of rostrum. BROWN sits centre.*)

BROWN: Good God.

TAFT: Tragic.

BROWN: Good God.

TAFT: Young life cut off –

BROWN: Does the Prime Minister know?

TAFT: Just like that.

WITHERS: No-one knows yet except ourselves.

BROWN: But what happened for heaven's sake, what went wrong?

WITHERS: The road block outside the city –

TAFT: Straight into it.

BROWN: What on earth was he doing?

WITHERS: About a hundred and twenty, sir.

BROWN: But what did he think he was doing? He must have seen it – it was a precaution!

TAFT: Just like his father.

BROWN: We cleared the whole damned motorway for him.

TAFT: Reckless. Grandfather. Same thing.

BROWN: What else did he want?

TAFT: Only that was a big, wild chestnut. Threw him and kicked his brains in.

BROWN: Was he mad, or what?

TAFT: Out, rather.

BROWN: But who in hell let him drive himself up?

WITHERS: He insisted, sir.

BROWN: You must be out of your minds. He's
    killed three people in that car in the last 18
    months, and you know it even if no-one else did.

WITHERS: You know how the public liked to see
    the Prince driving fast cars – the speed-loving
    Prince they called him.

TAFT: Hopeless horseman!

BROWN: I just can't get this into my mind. Is
    he really –

WITHERS: Instantly, sir.

BROWN: Good God.
    (*They stand in the stillness of the Cathedral, broken slightly*
    by the heavy breathing of the bearded CAMERAMAN, who
    has dropped off to sleep.)
    (*Passionately.*) Oh, you brainless, bloody, reckless,
    royal nit! (*His rage crumbles almost immediately to*
    near tears.)

TAFT: (*With contempt.*) Mr Brown, you
    forget yourself.

BROWN: Oh dear, yes. Forgive me, I didn't think
    what I was saying.

TAFT: I think we must remember who we are and
    our responsibilities at this moment.

BROWN: I was so upset I didn't know what I
    was saying.

TAFT: Naturally. A tragedy has happened. We must
    keep our heads, stifle our grief and decide what
    we must do.

BROWN: Tell me, what have you done with him?

WITHERS: He's outside.

BROWN: (*Frantic.*) Outside!

WITHERS: In Colonel Taft's car, sir.

BROWN: Car?

WITHERS: Yes, in the boot, sir.

BROWN: (*Rises.*) Boot! You can't leave a Prince of
    the Royal House in the boot!

TAFT: I was about to issue an order. Wimple's lot
    should have left by now. Withers, go and see and
    then instruct the guard.

WITHERS: Yes, sir. (*Goes.*)

TAFT: Look here, I suppose you realise what this means.

BROWN: Yes, another damn funeral. I haven't even ordered a new gun carriage.

TAFT: No, not that, surely, sir, I don't have to point out to you the possible consequences of this tragedy.

BROWN: Quite honestly, I haven't managed to work it out yet. The implications are too tremendous.

TAFT: Exactly. They'll be looking for a scapegoat.

BROWN: Oh, God!

TAFT: There will be accusations, charges of negligence. Could bring down the Government.

BROWN: We baptised him and allowed the sky to open, we let the white dove settle on him and what are we left with in the end?

TAFT: Eh?

BROWN: The King can't last much longer.

TAFT: Afraid not.

BROWN: Good God, man, there's no-one to take his place.

TAFT: Whose?

BROWN: The Prince's – Prince Wilhelm, of course.

TAFT: I am afraid I don't understand you, the line of succession is indisputable.

BROWN: You're really mad, Taft. Thank God we took over!

TAFT: His younger brother is his rightful successor and –

BROWN: Prince Heinrich!

TAFT: Prince Heinrich!

BROWN: Taft, Prince Heinrich is as queer as a cucumber.

TAFT: Queer?

BROWN: Yes, Taft, queer. You've been in this game 40 years, haven't you?

TAFT: Sir –

BROWN: Ginger beer, Taft, pansy, one of *those,* cissy. *Compris?* Bent!

TAFT: Good Lord, young Harry.

BROWN: Young Harry, he says – he's as bent as a bloody boomerang!

TAFT: Bent, but do you mean –

BROWN: Well?

TAFT: Well – that, that he'd never get married?

BROWN: Married – tough luck on *that* poor kid.

TAFT: But surely, sir, for the sake of his country, his duty –

BROWN: Taft, I don't know who you talk to in your job, but has it never struck you as slightly odd, even for a young Prince, that he should divide his time almost exclusively between the barracks and visiting the ballet.

TAFT: Well, naturally I thought that going to the theatre was a bit eccentric.

BROWN: And the grace and favour lavished on all those interior decorators and fashion photographers?

TAFT: I always thought they were utterly unsuitable companions for –

BROWN: Yes, yes, exactly. Well, there you are, you see; it's been me, old Joe Brown, I've been the one who has had to see that these things have been kept quiet.

TAFT: I'd no idea.

BROWN: Yes, that's bloody obvious, isn't it? Anyway, even if we can drag him up the aisle, who do you think we could get to go with him? Have you any idea at all how many eligible young women there are left in the whole of Europe?

TAFT: Let me think, well, there's –

BROWN: Yes, you have a jolly good think because I have.

TAFT: Well, it is difficult when you're suddenly – Princess Mariana?

BROWN: Mariana?

TAFT: Yes, you know, the Stettin-Bambergs.

BROWN: Stettin-Bambergs? Nobody will speak to them even in their own country.

TAFT: There's always Princess Theresa.

BROWN: They couldn't raise enough credit to put a deposit on a TV set to watch the wedding.

TAFT: Well, of course, if it's simply money you're talking about –

BROWN: You know it isn't. If it were worth it we'd pay them anything.

TAFT: Well, then –

BROWN: It's no use, Taft. Do you think I've not gone into it? Even if we could talk Prince Heinrich into it there isn't anyone available who isn't half dead, dotty or just plain unacceptable outside a waxworks.

TAFT: Have you ever considered Isabella, the Grand Duchess of –

BROWN: Yes, I have. She has to shave twice a day so she'd be able to use the Prince's razor, seeing that he doesn't have to.

TAFT: I think that's a very cruel, distasteful thing to say.

BROWN: She wears a surgical boot as big as a suitcase. Oh yes, she'd look great creeping up the aisle.

TAFT: But when the Prince succeeds, surely the thought of his duty – to the Royal House, the succession – he could, well, manage the once.

BROWN: He mustn't.

TAFT: But he'll be King.

BROWN: Or Queen.

TAFT: God, you're right.

BROWN: Heirs, Taft. There must be heirs. You know – and Salmon begat Booze of Rachab; and Booze begat Obed of Ruth; and Obed begat

Jessie; and with *these* two at least we could have began the begat all right. Believe me, we need to. Wilhelm may have been a long drink of watery milk but that girl Melanie, she'd have laid eggs like a cod-fish.

TAFT: I say, poor girl, what's going to happen to her now?

BROWN: (*Sadistically.*) Well, there'll be no performance for her tomorrow, or tomorrow night for that matter.

TAFT: But there is got to be – I –

BROWN: (*Takes TAFT's hand and pats it.*) I know what you mean, old man, I'm sorry I barked at you.

TAFT: No, not at all.

BROWN: But what can we do with her? This really looks like the end.

(*The body of PRINCE WILHELM is brought in by the guards, accompanied by WITHERS. It is placed in the centre of the stage. They all stare at it in silence and one by one go to look at it.*)

TAFT: (*Roughly.*) Well, there it is, the blood royal. (*WITHERS is the first to look at the PRINCE. While the others do the same he stares at the sleeping figure of the bearded CAMERAMAN. He goes over to him and examines him.*)

BROWN: Yes, it's the end alright. The end of everything as we know it.

TAFT: Bamberg blood. Well, we'd better keep him out of sight for the moment. (*To GUARD.*) You – cover him up. We've got to think, and think pretty hard.

BROWN: We might as well face up to it, Taft, it's all over. A big dream, a great idea, no –

TAFT: Oh, damn it, man, take hold of yourself for heaven's sake. Try and remember you're still one of His Majesty's Ministers. If you tell me what to do, I promise I'll carry it out.

WITHERS: Colonel Taft, sir.

TAFT: What is it? (*Crosses to WITHERS.*)

WITHERS: There's a man lying over here.

TAFT: What? Where? Where is he?

BROWN: A man. (*Rushes to the altar.*) Oh, my God, he's been listening.

TAFT: Good heavens, you're panicking again. Sit down for a moment. Let me look at him.

(*BROWN is too miserable to investigate and together TAFT and WITHERS stare at the sleeping man, who has traces of a smile around his mouth.*)

Do you think he is really asleep?

WITHERS: Either that or drunk, sir. A bit of both I should say. I have been watching him for the last minute or so.

TAFT: Withers.

WITHERS: Yes, sir.

(*TAFT leans right down and examines the man more closely.*)

TAFT: Withers, have you noticed –

WITHERS: Yes I have.

TAFT: Am I mad?

WITHERS: No sir, absolutely not.

TAFT: It's fantastic.

WITHERS: I know, I couldn't believe it myself. That's why I waited.

TAFT: What a resemblance!

WITHERS: The Bamberg nose, the Bamberg ears –

TAFT: Why, shave off that hideous beard and, and –

WITHERS: Prince Wilhelm, sir.

TAFT: The Prince.

WITHERS: Dressed as a cameraman.

TAFT: I wonder what his chin is like.

WITHERS: (*Encouragingly.*) Bearded men always have feeble chins, sir.

TAFT: That's why he grew it, I suppose.

WITHERS: Exactly, sir.

(*BROWN moans.*)

What are we going to do with the Minister, sir?

TAFT: Ah, yes. Well, I think we should collect our thoughts a bit, don't you. Get rid of him, put him in my car and tell him to go straight to the Palace and get himself a brandy or something. We'll fetch him later.

WITHERS: Yes, sir. (*He goes to BROWN and helps him up.*)

TAFT: Oh, and tell him to talk to no-one, understand, no-one.

WITHERS: Yes, Colonel Taft.

(*BROWN takes a last look at the corpse and is helped out by WITHERS. TAFT leans down again and studies the man's features in detail. Suddenly the man opens his eyes.*)

TAFT: (*Startled.*) Oh!

MAN: Phew! (*Pause.*) I don't know what you're yelling about, *you* scared *me.*

TAFT: I beg your pardon.

MAN· You can kill people like that, you know. If I had a weak heart you might have killed me.

TAFT: Yes, well, thank God, I didn't. Who are you?

MAN: I think I might ask you that except – except that I know who you are. You're Colonel Taft. I've had enough trouble with your office too many times not to know you.

TAFT: Come along, man, don't mess about. Who are you?

MAN: Are you asking for my Press Card?

TAFT: Yes, please.

MAN: Just as you like. (*Goes to pocket.*) I've got every right to be here, you know.

TAFT: What were you doing here?

MAN: I should have thought you'd have noticed that.

TAFT: Yes, I mean before.

MAN: I was setting up my cameras. For one thing, you boys wouldn't let me in until it was nearly too late, so I had a few drinks while I was kept hanging around, thanks to you again, and by the time I had been allowed to set up I just felt so flaked out, I sat down for a smoke and dropped off.

TAFT: (*Reading.*) Alan Russell. Photographer –
Australian United Press. Are these the people
you work for?

RUSSELL: Only on this one. I work for myself.

TAFT: Come over here a minute will you, please?

RUSSELL: What do you mean? I'll be finished in
a couple of minutes. You don't have to throw
your weight around, you know.

TAFT: Do shut up for a minute, man. Come in the
light where I can see you.
(*RUSSELL allows himself to be shifted into the light and
peered at.*)

RUSSELL: Top lighting makes me look better, but
it's not very good in here.

TAFT: It's good enough.
(*Enter WITHERS.*)
Withers, look – look at him.
(*WITHERS comes up and examines RUSSELL.*)

WITHERS: Remarkable, absolutely remarkable.
(*RUSSELL looks puzzled but slightly amused. He is
a good-humoured man.*)

RUSSELL: If I smoke will it spoil your view?

TAFT: What? No, certainly.
(*WITHERS smartly offers RUSSELL a cigarette.*)

RUSSELL: Oh, thank you. Must be quite a strain
for you boys, a job like this.

TAFT: Mr Russell, where do you come from?

RUSSELL: Well, I've shown you my card. Australia.

TAFT: Yes, but has your family always lived
in Australia?

RUSSELL: Pretty well, I suppose.

TAFT: I mean, do you have any family connections
in Europe?

RUSSELL: Sure.

TAFT: Look, Russell, what does the name Bamberg
mean to you?

RUSSELL: Just about what it does to you
I should say.

TAFT: Nothing more?

RUSSELL: Well, I used to think it was a bit of
a joke when I was a kid.

TAFT: A joke, what kind of a joke?

RUSSELL: Well, you see, Bamberg was a name
I often used to hear when I was a little kid.
Sometimes I'd hear my old man rowing with
my mother and somehow that name was always
coming up and whenever it did, sure enough
my mother would end up in tears and poor old
Dad would storm out of the house.

TAFT: Go on.

RUSSELL: The last time I saw him, just before he
died, I heard him shouting – "There you are you
see, that's your son, there's the bloody Bamberg
coming out in him!" I'd just been sick on the
bathroom floor and on that particular occasion
I wasn't sure if he'd said Hamburg or hamburger
or something. My mother's family came from
somewhere near Hamburg, you see.

TAFT: Hamburg, yes.

RUSSELL: So it was a bit confusing, especially at
the time.

TAFT: Did you ever ask your mother about
Bamberg?

RUSSELL: Well I didn't, as a matter of fact, until
after Dad died. Because, well the name seemed
to upset him too much and I didn't like to ask,
but later I did say to her one day – "Who is this
Mr Bamberg?"

TAFT: What did she say to that?

RUSSELL: She said – "He was a very dear friend
of your mother's when she was on holiday in
Europe once."

TAFT: When was this?

RUSSELL: What – Bamberg? The holiday? Oh,
just before she got married, I think.

TAFT: (*To WITHERS.*) It is, it is.

WITHERS: What was your mother's name?

TAFT: Walters?

RUSSELL: Walters – how did you know my
mother's name?

TAFT: I remember her. She was a pretty little thing,
blonde, very blonde. That's why I remember her.
She was the only blonde he ever had. It was
a relief after all those pasty-looking brunettes
and red-heads.

RUSSELL: This job's really gone to your heads,
I think.

TAFT: I apologise, Mr Russell. You shall have an
explanation. Come over here.
(*He takes RUSSELL to the body, centre. WITHERS
uncovers it.*)

RUSSELL: Phew! Oh, I say, what about that, eh?
You boys are in trouble, I guess.
(*Both men are watching RUSSELL.*)
Gosh, he's a mess, isn't he? You know, I never
realised he'd got such big ears. Yes – hey, you
know, put a beard on him and he'd look a bit
like me.
(*TAFT nods to WITHERS.*)

WITHERS: Mr Russell, would you mind coming
with me?

RUSSELL: Why? Where?

WITHERS: Oh, just to the Palace.

RUSSELL: To the Palace, what for?

WITHERS: For a shave, Mr Russell, for a shave.

End of Act One.

ACT TWO

Scene 1

A room in the Palace.

RUSSELL, clean-shaven and wearing full dress uniform with sword and decorations, is kneeling before a long mirror. WITHERS and TAFT look on.

TAFT: ... Amen.

RUSSELL: Hey! But, do I have to stay on my knees all this time?

TAFT: Oh, don't grumble any more for heaven's sake.

WITHERS: There'll be a faldstool, your Royal Highness.

RUSSELL: A what?

WITHERS: A cushion.

RUSSELL: (*Sitting.*) Grumble, he says! I should think I've got something to grumble about. I can't keep my eyes open.

WITHERS: Have some more black coffee.
(*He rings.*)

TAFT: Good heavens, man! What's the matter with you?

RUSSELL: A good question. I can't remember my lines, and I can't stop this bloody sword swinging between my legs.

TAFT: Where's your manhood?

RUSSELL: Doing alright till this morning, thank you, mate.

WITHERS: (*Encouragingly.*) You're doing splendidly. Another couple of times through the whole ceremony and you'll be perfect. You only forgot three things last time.

TAFT: Those three were enough to bring the country to a standstill.

RUSSELL: Well, as far as I'm concerned, you can send for somebody else.

TAFT: There *is* no-one else.

RUSSELL: Look: I'm not used to giving orders to a butler, let alone being a royal bridegroom.

WITHERS: Don't worry, old man. I'll get the Archbishop to cue you in all the way through. (*To TAFT.*) He can get him through it. (*To RUSSELL.*) I'll say you've got a bad attack of first-night nerves.

RUSSELL: First night – don't talk to me about *that*!

TAFT: (*Grimly.*) No, I should wait till you come to it, my friend.

RUSSELL: *If* I come to it. My friend, you're no friend to me. You'd better get yourself another boy.

TAFT: I've told you: it's you or nothing.

RUSSELL: Then it'll have to be nothing, that's all. I'm certainly not marrying a princess I've never even been introduced to.

TAFT: It won't be nothing, Russell, because I shan't let it be nothing. There's too much at stake. I'm warning you. You are unimportant to me. You are nobody. As I am. As we all are.

RUSSELL: (*Breaks towards TAFT.*) Are you threatening me?

TAFT: If you wish.

RUSSELL: Listen, all I've got to do is holler and get out of here.

TAFT: (*Quietly.*) You'll not get out alive. (*TAFT takes out a revolver.*)

RUSSELL: (*Backs away.*) You're mad.

TAFT: Maybe. I've been living in a mad world for a long time. Longer than either of you.
(*There is a knock at the door. TAFT puts away his pistol unhurriedly. A FOOTMAN enters.*)

WITHERS: His Royal Highness would like another pot of black coffee.

(*The FOOTMAN bows and goes out. There is a tense pause.*)

TAFT: I'm sorry, Russell.

RUSSELL: That's alright. (*To WITHERS.*) Would he have done it?

(*WITHERS nods.*)

TAFT: I was overcome.

RUSSELL: Sure.

TAFT: There is so much at stake. For all of us. Think again, my dear chap. Please think again. Don't be hasty.

RUSSELL: Alright.

TAFT: An entire world is involved. All that we have left. It's precious little.

RUSSELL: I'm beginning to see that.

TAFT: You're not a man to be threatened.

RUSSELL: Or bribed?

TAFT: Just think – think of the responsibility that lies in your hands at this moment.

RUSSELL: Well?

TAFT: A whole way of life. We are its servants, instruments of order, decency and all the things that have made life honourable and tolerable for a thousand years.

RUSSELL: I need time to think about it.

TAFT: There isn't any time. And the one thing you mustn't do is think. You must act, and be what you are.

RUSSELL: I've never had to make that decision.

TAFT: Make it now.

RUSSELL: How much longer have we got?

WITHERS: Six hours and 22 minutes.

RUSSELL: Alright, then, let's go through the drill again. From the top.

WITHERS: I should wait for your coffee, Your Royal Highness.

TAFT: Yes, yes, take a rest for a bit. You've time yet. We'll get through.

(*A knock at the door. The FOOTMAN enters with coffee.*)

WITHERS: Ah, here we are. Get this lot down –
Your Royal Highness. Is there anything else
you'd like?

RUSSELL: Eh? No. Oh yes, I think I will. I'll have
– I'll have a bottle of brandy and some soda.

TAFT: (*Under breath.*) Careful now.

RUSSELL: And, and – don't go. It's getting light.
I might as well eat while I'm at it. I think I'll
have bacon and eggs.

FOOTMAN: Very good, Your Royal Highness.

RUSSELL: And toast and marmalade.

TAFT: Excellent idea. We'll all have some.

RUSSELL: Good.

WITHERS: (*To FOOTMAN.*) Soon as you can.

FOOTMAN: I'll have to wake –

RUSSELL: Then wake 'em! Wake the lot! After all,
it is my goddam wedding day, is it not?
(*The FOOTMAN bows and goes out. TAFT and WITHERS
exchange relieved glances.*)

WITHERS: Well now, that sounds better!

RUSSELL: I'm not convinced, mind. But
I'm interested.

TAFT: Good man! (*Throws prayer book on to pouffe.*)

RUSSELL: Or I'm prepared to be. Interest me.
(*TAFT glares at him outraged.*)

TAFT: Interest you! Good heavens, man, we're not
selling you a spin dryer or something.

RUSSELL: You'd better start trying.

TAFT: Damn it, you're being offered one of the –
of the purest, most perfect pearls of living. It's
like redemption; it can't be bought or bargained
for. It is impossible to offer you anything
more valuable.

RUSSELL: At a price.

TAFT: What do you mean, price? What price?

RUSSELL: Well, my freedom for instance.

TAFT: Freedom? *Your* freedom? What's that
worth precisely?

RUSSELL: At this moment, precisely, I'd say its market value had never been higher.

TAFT: Damn your freedom, man. You can live without that. Tell me: what about duty? Eh? What about duty? That's harder to live without.

RUSSELL: (*Baffled for the moment.*) What about – work?

TAFT: Her Royal Highness will be your work.

RUSSELL: Yes, well. Maybe she'll be *too* hard work.

TAFT: She's exacting.

RUSSELL: But how satisfying?

TAFT: There'll be rewards. More than you ever got before.

RUSSELL: I wish you wouldn't say "got before" like that.

TAFT: Well, come along, my friend, let's be frank. You're not a great artist or something, someone whose work is so important to them.

RUSSELL: No. That's quite true. But I'm good at it.

TAFT: But no more.

RUSSELL: And I enjoy it. Still, I daresay they'd manage without me.

TAFT: Come: a princess is more than a fair return for *that*.

RUSSELL: We'll come round to her later. What do I get?

TAFT: Get?

RUSSELL: Loot.

TAFT: Eh?

WITHERS: He wants a breakdown, sir, of the Prince's personal fortune.

RUSSELL: And the Princess's.

TAFT: Oh, do come along!

RUSSELL: Oh, alright. By the way, I warn you: I can't get on a horse, shoot, play polo, or handle a yacht.

WITHERS: Oh Lord!

RUSSELL: Nor am I prepared to.

TAFT: Rubbish! You'll have to.

RUSSELL: I might, however, open the occasional industrial exhibition, or launch an obsolete ocean liner. You know, I've always wanted to crack a bottle of champagne against one of those things.

(*TAFT looks as if he might take out his revolver again.*)

WITHERS: I'm glad you're beginning to come round to our point of view. You see, Russell – Your Royal Highness – your personal fortune at this time is not vast, although by the standards of most men, it is very considerable.

RUSSELL: How much?

WITHERS: In your private purse, probably no more than a quarter of a million –

RUSSELL: Is that all?

WITHERS: Your income, however, added to the Princess's, would be very large indeed.

RUSSELL: How much?

TAFT: Withers!

WITHERS: Well, as a full-time, working Prince of the Royal House, you will naturally have an allowance from the public purse.

TAFT: Reviewable annually by Parliament.

WITHERS: After an event such as your wedding, they will almost certainly do something ordinarily unpopular, like cutting the schools programme and increase your allowance.

RUSSELL: Good.

(*TAFT sits on pouffe.*)

WITHERS: And at such time as the Princess should produce an heir, there would be similar arrangements.

RUSSELL: Excellent.

WITHERS: Your father, as you may know, was a friendly, dissolute man who squandered a vast sum of money before he died, mostly on horses and opera singers – an especially rich product of your own country, I believe. Your mother, however, was a sensible thrifty woman, who, apart from furnishing all your royal residences at wisely invested expense "and with *monumental* vulgarity", made the widest possible provision for any of her sons who might follow in their father's footsteps. All Your Royal Highness's capital has been shrewdly invested in a large number of places, all of them assured, safe and profitable. Apart from your mother's stupendously valuable collection of antique junk, with which, however, you will be compelled to live, there is her jewellery, considered to be beyond value; your collection of paintings, from Holbein to Sickert, most of them rather dull but priceless, which has been recently valued by one popular newspaper at nearly two million pounds. You have a royal residence in the capital, of course, which is rather like an enormous version of one of the older, famous, Edwardian hotels. You have a seat in the provinces which is reasonably comfortable. The weather is not good usually, and you will have to stride about in a thick rubber macintosh and gum boots, which will make you popular with one certain, unconsidered section of the population. Twice on Sundays, you will go to the local church, and sit interminably in your pew with the rest of the crowded congregation to prove how democratic you are. It is a little like attending one of the flashier film premieres in a small village, but you will soon learn to accept it as part of your country life timetable. You also own a huge Gothic obscenity in the north, which is like a plush railway station with William Morris wallpaper. But it's very popular with the people, so you are obliged to visit it during the summer, when you're expected to dress in the very quaint local costume, and pretend that you are not yourselves foreigners. This is to encourage the inhabitants of that sentimentally fierce province not to insist on their sovereignty, which they are very relieved not to have to do anyway. For this service, the Government pays the whole crippling upkeep of the place, and bribes you in return for your claustrophobic and overwhelming boredom.

RUSSELL: Go on.

WITHERS: In addition to this, you're one of the nation's greatest landowners, the richest of large-scale farmers and breeders and racehorse owners – all at no effort to yourself. You derive income and increments from ancient lands, sources and foundations that everyone but the dustiest bookkeepers had forgotten. In short, Your Royal Highness, you are good and loaded.

RUSSELL: Yes. I see. (*He plays absently with his sword. Pause.*)

TAFT: Well?

RUSSELL: Well –

(*FOOTMAN enters with a trolley.*)

I suppose I'd better take a look at her.

TAFT: Take – !

RUSSELL: I mean I ought to see what it is exactly I'm getting.

WITHERS: (*To FOOTMAN.*) Leave that for the moment.

RUSSELL: After all, I've only seen her on newsreels –

FOOTMAN: Yes, sir.

WITHERS: Ah, but she's damaged her fetlock since then, Your Royal Highness. She's not the same animal.

TAFT: Quite.

(*Exit FOOTMAN.*)

Now, look here, Russell –

RUSSELL: I tell you – no see, no deal.

TAFT: There's no time.

RUSSELL: I only want to talk to her for five minutes. After all, I'm the one who's going to be stuck with her. Besides, she may not fancy the idea herself.

TAFT: The Princess has been brought up all her life with an immaculate understanding of duty and honour. She'll not shirk her responsibilities.

RUSSELL: Well, I might shirk mine. Have you told her yet?

TAFT: No.

RUSSELL: But you were going to?

TAFT: Yes, of course. I was going to tell her. Her Royal Highness is no fool, even if you might like to think so. She'd have got your number in half a minute. Come to think of it, Russell, I'm not even sure if you're capable of seeing it through. Perhaps we're asking too much of you.

RUSSELL: The price is high, but I'm still interested.

TAFT: But can you do it? As you say yourself, you're not born to it. It has to be in the blood.

RUSSELL: Colonel Taft, I shall do my best.

TAFT: Hm. Well, we've no choice. I'd better go and break the news to Her Royal Highness. Have some breakfast, learn your lines, study that plan of the ceremony, and keep your mouth shut in front of the servants. Come on, Withers, you'd better come too. Oh, by the way, the Princess is a very devout young woman. You do believe in God, don't you?

RUSSELL: Not necessarily.

TAFT: Oh, well, she'll just have to believe for both of you. At least try to look as though you believed in that sword a bit.

(*He and WITHERS go out. RUSSELL mimes a little with his sword, then gives up. He tries kneeling and walking up the aisle. He practises a Royal Walk, a Royal Handshake, a Royal Tour of a factory. He is just about to launch an ocean liner – "And may God bless all who sail in her" – when the*

FOOTMAN and two others come back into the room with breakfast. They lay and prepare it, while he does his best to look nonchalant.)

RUSSELL: *(Finally.)* That'll – *(Regaining his vocal register.)* – that'll do. Colonel Taft and Captain Withers will have theirs presently. I'll have mine now.

FOOTMAN: Very good, Your Royal Highness.

(The other two go out, and RUSSELL sits down while he is served by the first FOOTMAN.)

Kidneys? *Your Royal Highness?*

RUSSELL: Yes, yes, yes. Please.

(RUSSELL looks cautiously at the smiling FOOTMAN as he waits on him.)

Er –

FOOTMAN: Yes, Your Royal Highness?

RUSSELL: Oh, nothing, nothing. That's all, thank you.

(Pause.)

You can go now.

FOOTMAN: Very good, Your Royal Highness. Perhaps Your Royal Highness was thinking he had seen me before?

RUSSELL: Well, I –

FOOTMAN: You see, like Your Royal Highness, I'm here on my Press Card too. *(He bows out.)*

RUSSELL: Oh, God! *(Finally, he shrugs and starts on his breakfast.)* Well – *(Lifts up silver dish.)* – live while it lasts!

(He starts to eat. As he does so a WOMAN suddenly bursts in through the door. She closes it behind her sharply, leaning against it, panting lightly. She is scarcely forty, wears a macintosh, a plastic head cover and carries a large bag, almost like a kit-bag.)

WOMAN: Oh!

RUSSELL: Who are *you?*

(The WOMAN stares unbelievingly at him.)

You! *(Grandly.)* What do you want?

WOMAN: Oh! Your *Highness!*

RUSSELL: Eh? You're not an assassin, are you? What are you doing here? Eh? How did you get into the Palace? You don't live here, surely?

WOMAN: Oh! Your Highness!

RUSSELL: Don't keep saying that. Where have you come from? (*Pause.*) You do speak English, do you? Where have you come from?

WOMAN: Well, I – I – Oh, Your Highness!

RUSSELL: Come over here. I'm trying to have my breakfast. What do you want?

WOMAN: I've been in the laundry chute, you see, Your Highness. Oh dear, I'm sure I look such a mess!

(*She steps forward, and takes off her mac, hat, etc. Underneath, she is wearing a reasonably smart, mass-produced dress with a quantity of cheap jewellery. From her bag, she takes high-heeled shoes, which she puts on, replacing the galoshes she has been wearing. She takes a sharp, distressed glance at herself in a hand mirror. RUSSELL is intrigued, but goes on with his breakfast.*)

RUSSELL: Why are you doing all that?

(*She ignores him, her concentration is so intense for the moment.*)

Well – think I'll take off my sword. (*He does so, placing it beside the dish of kidneys.*) What have you been doing in the laundry chute? Is that why your dress is slightly creased?

WOMAN: Oh! Is it? Where? Where? Show me! No, you can't! Oh, dear! Oh, dear!

(*RUSSELL watches her, as, obsessed and absorbed, she studies and rearranges herself. He decides she's harmless, and, studying the plan of the Cathedral and the royal route, gets on with eating his breakfast. Finally, the WOMAN decides that there is no more she can do about her appearance, and, after carefully arranging her macintosh and bag on a chair, she steps forward uncertainly. RUSSELL ignores her. She coughs, putting all the gentility she can make into it. There is no response, so she comes a few steps downstage and repeats it. RUSSELL looks up.*)

RUSSELL: You can't read a map, can you?

WOMAN: No, Your Highness, I'm afraid I
can't actually –

RUSSELL: No? Well, it's not so much a map as
a plan –

WOMAN: (*Eagerly.*) Oh! Is it a plan of the Royal
Route? I cut mine out of the papers days ago.

RUSSELL: Did you? Then perhaps you'd explain
this one to me.

WOMAN: Oh, really! May I?

RUSSELL: Sure.

WOMAN: *May* I? Your Royal Highness?

RUSSELL: If you wouldn't mind –

WOMAN: Mind!

RUSSELL: You look a little bit odd. Are
you   alright?

WOMAN: Your Highness! I'm more alright at this
moment than I've ever been in my entire life!

RUSSELL: Perhaps you'd like a cup of coffee? (*She
nods.*) Hang on. (*He is just about to pour a cup,
and then hesitates.*) I'll call the footman.

WOMAN: Oh, no! Don't do that!

RUSSELL: Why not?

WOMAN: Oh, don't do that, I beg of you, Your
Highness; don't give me away!

RUSSELL: Away?

WOMAN: Nobody knows I'm here –

RUSSELL: Ah, yes –

WOMAN: You don't know what I've been through
for this moment! How I've waited and waited,
and longed – and prayed to God and thought –

RUSSELL: How long were you in the laundry chute?

WOMAN: Two days.

RUSSELL: What? Were you buried under the royal
laundry, I suppose?

WOMAN: Yes! (*Rapturously.*) For two whole days and
nights! But even that was wonderful. It was worth
all the planning and sacrifice, Your Highness.
I just lay there, breathing it in, and, do you

know, I could have stayed there for ever. I felt
a sense of peace and contentment and well-being
in that place, under all your dirty clothes, like
I've never known in my life before.

RUSSELL: Would you like a brandy with your coffee?

WOMAN: Oh, thanks very much, Your Highness.
Bit early in the day for me – but, well, in
the circumstances –

RUSSELL: How did you know this was my room?

WOMAN: Oh, I know this place like the back of
my hand. I know where you all live and eat and
sleep, and –

RUSSELL: But, tell me, dirty laundry, as such,
doesn't have any special attraction for you?

WOMAN: Certainly not! There's nothing like that
about me. I'm a married woman.

RUSSELL: Children?

WOMAN: Three, Your Highness. Renee, that's
my eldest, she'll be 17 next month, and then
Gloria, she's just 14. And the boy, Anthony,
he's eight.

RUSSELL: Yes?

WOMAN: Yes. He's the youngest.

RUSSELL: You mean the other two are older?

WOMAN: That's right, Your Highness.

RUSSELL: But does your husband know where
you are?

WOMAN: Well, he doesn't know exactly where I am.
(*Giggles.*) He'd have a shock if he saw me having
a drop of brandy at this time of the morning! He's
not a drinker himself, you see – I mean, he doesn't
mind those who do, but he never does himself. It
has no appeal to him.

RUSSELL: What does appeal to him?

WOMAN: Well, he's pretty keen on the football, and
the television quite often – though he won't
watch the plays. He'll go out of the room if I put
a play on.

RUSSELL: What's he doing now?

WOMAN: Oh, he's minding the children.

RUSSELL: And he's quite happy to do that, is he?

WOMAN: He doesn't mind. He's used to it. He'll help get them their teas when he's at home, and when he's not, Renee's a very good girl, she does it. His hours are a bit irregular. He's an inspector on the buses, you see. So he's very busy just now, what with all the crowds and that.

RUSSELL: But he doesn't mind you going off, and disappearing for a few days at a time?

WOMAN: Oh, my goodness, no! (*She laughs.*) Old Bill doesn't care much about anything really. You can't ruffle him, not even if you was to tell him the world was coming to an end! Oh, dear, Your Highness, I do hope you'll forgive me, but I think your brandy's gone to my head a bit –

RUSSELL: Have some more –

WOMAN: Oh, no –

RUSSELL: On the House – of Bamberg –

WOMAN: Oh, no, I couldn't, really –
(*He pours some.*)
Well, I suppose just a little drop then. After all, it's a real occasion for me; this doesn't happen to me every day. (*Passionately.*) Oh, Your Highness! (*She breaks off as though she might suddenly cry. RUSSELL begins to look alarmed.*)

RUSSELL: Perhaps you ought to have some breakfast –

WOMAN: Yes, well you might be right! I haven't had much for two days, apart from a few sardine sandwiches and a tomato.

RUSSELL: You had those in the laundry chute?

WOMAN: Yes.

RUSSELL: (*Helping her to breakfast.*) Allow me.

WOMAN: Oh, no, I couldn't – please, you mustn't. Well, oh dear, well thank you, thank you very much. Yes, that'll do very nicely. Oh, kidneys!

Oh, how nice! Oh, what a surprise! I feel as if I'm dreaming. (*She giggles again.*) But I'm not. I'm not dreaming, am I, Your Highness? It's real, all absolutely real. I'm sitting with the Prince, His Royal Highness, in the Palace, having bacon and eggs.

RUSSELL: And kidneys.

WOMAN: And kidneys! And brandy! Oh, I wish my friend could see me now. She'll never believe it. (*She giggles again and drops a slice of bacon into her lap.*) Oh, dear, now look what I've done! No, please don't get up, Your Highness. Please! It's my own fault. Oh dear, I am awful. It's that drop of brandy I expect. (*Suddenly very cross.*) Oh damn! All down my best dress!

RUSSELL: Have another. (*Rises with decanter.*)

WOMAN: I can't go out and buy one now.

RUSSELL: (*Handing her another rasher and a drink.*) Here.

WOMAN: Oh well, we only live once, as they say.

RUSSELL: That's right. It's a great day for both of us. Here's to it.

WOMAN: Cheers!

RUSSELL: Good luck!

WOMAN: (*In a soft whisper.*) Your Highness.
(*They eat, but the WOMAN, inflamed by the brandy, cannot take her eyes off him. Presently he begins to feel the strain.*)

RUSSELL: You don't think Bill's concerned about you?

WOMAN: (*Wearily.*) Oh, Bill.

RUSSELL: You don't think you ought to give him a ring?

WOMAN: No.

RUSSELL: I suppose he's used to your going off?

WOMAN: He just thinks I've taken up my usual place outside the Palace. That's my sleeping-bag I've got in there, you see.

RUSSELL: You seem quite well equipped.

WOMAN: And my little stove, and my transistor, magazines and blankets, in case it gets a bit chilly. Oh, I'm an old hand, Your Highness. (*Suddenly almost collapsing with emotion.*) Oh, Your Highness.

RUSSELL: (*Staving her off.*) But, tell me – just exactly how did you get into the Palace?

WOMAN: When I think of you –

RUSSELL: You must have been very determined.

WOMAN: You and your *bride*! (*She seems to put all the emotion of her lifetime into the word "bride".*)

RUSSELL: Security must be pretty ropy.

WOMAN: Your *magnificent* bride!

RUSSELL: Do you think so?

WOMAN: Oh – *Your Highness*. (*She stares at him with fierce sexual longing, and her face begins to harden.*)

RUSSELL: You don't seem to be eating your kidneys. Are they alright?

WOMAN: It's no good.

RUSSELL: Shall I send for some more?

WOMAN: I couldn't eat a thing.

RUSSELL: I'll ring for the footman –

WOMAN: No, don't do that! I can't do anything while you're in the room.

RUSSELL: I think perhaps you ought to go. You're looking –
(*She throws herself on to her knees and moans wildly.*)

WOMAN: Your Highness!
(*Horrified, he tries to help her to her feet, but she hurls herself at his boots in a rugby tackle.*)
No, no, you mustn't – please, Your Highness. I beg you, you mustn't. Your Royal Highness, my Highness, forgive me! Forgive me!
(*Ecstatically she kisses his polished boots.*)

RUSSELL: I forgive you alright. Now, why don't you –

WOMAN: Don't ridicule me.

RUSSELL: I'm not –

WOMAN: Don't ridicule me!

RUSSELL: I just –

WOMAN: I love you. You're all I ever think about. I love you. I am your most humble, I'm your most loving subject. I just love you. I worship you. I love you. You are my one and only god. Oh, Your Highness! Have a little pity.
(*RUSSELL looks down into her face, contorted with raw desire.*)
(*In a whisper.*) You know what I want. You can see it, can't you? (*RUSSELL nods.*) I'm prepared to die for you. I mean it. Just for a few precious moments. Less. (*There is an ugly challenge in her glance. And she leaps up and goes over to her bag.*) All right, if you don't believe me – oh, where is it? Damn! Just a minute – ah! (*She brings out a large obsolete-looking pistol.*)

RUSSELL: What are you doing with that thing?

WOMAN: It's a *souvenir*. Bill took it off a dead officer in the war.

RUSSELL: Well, put it away.

WOMAN: Oh no, Your Highness, my darling, my darling, my only real darling, I have to call you that. I couldn't shoot at you. That – that would be like trying to shoot at God. (*Hopelessly.*) You see?

RUSSELL: I do now.

WOMAN: Your Highness –
(*Pause. She eyes him like a snake about to strike and advances slowly towards him.*)
If you don't – if you don't – if you don't do what I – what I desire – (*She's said it now, so she repeats the word more hungrily than ever.*) what I desire more than anything else in this world – I shall turn this gun on myself, so help me God, I will –

RUSSELL: On yourself?

WOMAN: Your Highness.

RUSSELL: Madam: I'm sorry but I must contain myself for my bride.

WOMAN: Oh God!

RUSSELL: Now, please put that thing away –

WOMAN: (*With triumph.*) I knew you'd say that! I knew it in my heart of hearts. After all, what else could you say?

RUSSELL: What? About my bride?

WOMAN: Your Princess. Your magnificent Princess. (*RUSSELL moves to her.*) Keep away!

RUSSELL: But, please listen, Mrs –

WOMAN: Mrs Robbins.

RUSSELL: Mrs Robbins.

WOMAN: I'm not fooling –

RUSSELL: Mrs Robbins, now don't be silly.

WOMAN: This is my whole life – in a few moments –

RUSSELL: But it isn't. It can't be. Think of Bill, and Renee and Gloria and – the youngest.

WOMAN: (*Calmer now.*) Please, Your Highness; I ask you, do not mock me. We little people, who watch, and worship, and lead our little, unimportant lives, we have our little place, our little dignity. I ask for one thing.

RUSSELL: Anything.

WOMAN: A kiss.

(*He moves to her.*)

No!

(*She goes to him as if she were the centre of some sacrificial procession, transfixed, like someone sleep-walking. He puts out his cheek, she ignores it, takes his hand, kneels, and kisses it lingeringly. RUSSELL tries to make a grab at her pistol, but she is too alert. She leaps back.*)

Keep back!

RUSSELL: Put that away.

WOMAN: You're too late. You're much, much too late, but it was worth it. *It was worth it.*

(*Putting the pistol to her head she shoots herself, slumping on to RUSSELL's foot. However, he manages to roll her off and grasps the nearest brandy. The FOOTMAN rushes in.*)

FOOTMAN: Phew! Who did it?

RUSSELL: What? She did, of course.

FOOTMAN: Who was she?

RUSSELL: How do I know?

FOOTMAN: Are these her things here?

RUSSELL: Yes. Her sleeping-bag. And transistor. Here, you can't go through her things like that. They're private.

FOOTMAN: Hm. Electricity bill and letter addressed to her. Mrs William Robbins. Children?

RUSSELL: Three. Here –

(*Enter TAFT and WITHERS.*)

TAFT: What's going on? Good heavens! Is she dead?

FOOTMAN: Yes, sir.

RUSSELL: She shot herself.

TAFT: Lunatic, I suppose.

RUSSELL: No. Just a loyal subject.

TAFT: Why did she shoot herself?

RUSSELL: She asked too much, too much from life and too much from me, in particular.

TAFT: Ah! (*To FOOTMAN.*) Here – you, take her outside, somewhere. Captain Withers will give you a hand.

WITHERS: Yes, sir.

TAFT: Only hurry. The Princess will be here in a minute.

(*WITHERS and the FOOTMAN collect up the WOMAN's belongings, pile them on to her body and are about to carry her off.*)

RUSSELL: Just a moment. What's that footman's name?

TAFT: Name?

WITHERS: Robert, isn't it?

TAFT: Come along, Your Royal Highness, there isn't –

RUSSELL: His name isn't Robert and he knows I'm not His Royal Highness.
(*The FOOTMAN stands holding one end of the WOMAN's body. Then, his face breaks into a smirk.*)

TAFT: Is this true?
(*The FOOTMAN nods.*)
I see.
(*TAFT takes out a small automatic and walks gravely towards the FOOTMAN, whose smirk freezes into disbelief, the WOMAN's body slipping from his hands. He looks around for escape, but WITHERS is already blocking the doorway.*)

FOOTMAN: There's nothing you can do, you know. You can't get away with this. (*Appealing to RUSSELL.*) Russell – tell him –
(*TAFT shoots, and the FOOTMAN drops dead beside the WOMAN.*)

TAFT: Poor devil! Shifty face though.

WITHERS: He was fairly new, I think.

RUSSELL: He was a journalist.

WITHERS: Journalist! Good Lord!

TAFT: Well, that's not so bad then, after all. Withers, you can tell Commodore Crabtree to issue a statement saying the woman shot him by mistake and then turned the gun on herself.
(*Enter PRINCESS MELANIE. She stares at the bodies.*)

MELANIE: Who are they?

TAFT: It's Robert, Your Royal Highness.

MELANIE: I can see that. It's that new, clumsy one.

TAFT: It seems, Your Royal Highness, he was really a journalist.

MELANIE: Well, that explains one or two things. And the woman?

TAFT: Lunatic.

MELANIE: Well, can't you get rid of them or something?

TAFT: Withers!

WITHERS: Yes, sir.

RUSSELL: Here, shall I give you a hand?

MELANIE: Don't be ridiculous. Stay where you are.
(*WITHERS drags out the bodies.*)

WITHERS: It's alright, Your Royal Highness.
I can manage.

MELANIE: And do close the door, for
heaven's sake! (*Sits.*)

RUSSELL: (*Weary and irritable by now.*) You're not
in a very pretty mood, are you?

MELANIE: The news is not exactly welcome –
Mr Russell.

RUSSELL: (*Relenting immediately.*) I'm sorry. Of
course, you must be very upset.

MELANIE: Upset! Of course I'm upset! What
stupid words you use. (*To TAFT.*) He's not very
intelligent, is he?
(*TAFT shrugs, humbly and helplessly.*)
Still, neither was poor Willy, but I was very fond
of him. The only time he ever put his foot down
was in those absurd sports cars. Oh! (*Her voice
breaks, more with frustration than deep sorrow.*)
And – you!

TAFT: (*To RUSSELL.*) Apart from breaking the
tragic news to Her Highness, I've also done my
best to outline the present situation, particularly
as it affects the Constitution and the country as
a whole. Unfortunately, personal grief for those
in exalted places cannot be allowed to –

MELANIE: Oh, really, Taft – you are the most
tiresome man in the entire world! Constitution
and country! Do you think I don't know all that
stuff backwards?

TAFT: (*Persisting gravely.*) Her country's honour
must at all times take precedence over her
personal grief, however bitter, however tragic.

MELANIE: (*Stamping her foot.*) Taft! If you say that
once more, I shall scream!

TAFT: I beg your pardon –

MELANIE: Oh, go away or something.

TAFT: Very good, Your Royal Highness.

MELANIE: I want to talk to this man. What's your name?

RUSSELL: Russell.

MELANIE: Russell.

TAFT: May I just remind you both of something important. Time is short. (*Goes out.*)

RUSSELL: He's right. It's almost light already. And I still haven't learnt my lines.

MELANIE: Russell –

RUSSELL: Colonel Taft seems to think there's some Bamberg stuffed away in me somewhere.

MELANIE: I must say you look extraordinarily like poor Willy.

RUSSELL: Thanks.

MELANIE: You're not to make me cry. This is quite difficult enough as it is.

RUSSELL: Sorry.

MELANIE: There's something – something indefinably insolent about you.

RUSSELL: (*Sits.*) I don't know any better.

MELANIE: You'll have to start learning. Do sit down. (*He rises – she sits.*) What makes you think you can impersonate someone like Willy?

RUSSELL: What you said: insolence, I guess. Anyhow, you don't have to go along with the idea if you don't like it.

MELANIE: Oh, don't be ridiculous.

RUSSELL: Eh?

MELANIE: I've no choice.

RUSSELL: Duty?

MELANIE: Yes, I suppose – you think that's very amusing. Why are *you* prepared to do it?

RUSSELL: For the loot.

MELANIE: Loot?

RUSSELL: Loot. Come on – you see home movies. I've read about it. You like musicals and light comedies.

MELANIE: Oh – money.

RUSSELL: Oh – money.

MELANIE: But do you mean you'll do anything for money? Anything?

RUSSELL: No, not anything.

MELANIE: What do you mean? And why do you have that weird accent?

RUSSELL: I've not had all that many offers. I might marry *you,* for instance –

MELANIE: Is it Australian?

RUSSELL: Yes. Mind you, that's for *real* loot.

MELANIE: Well, it's quite hideous.

RUSSELL: The loot?

MELANIE: No, your accent. You'll have to try and say as little as possible for the first few days. Or you can pretend it's one of his – your – tiresome jokes.

RUSSELL: I see. I make tiresome jokes, do I?

MELANIE: Constantly. Willy was just a schoolboy – everyone knew that. And don't say "loot" again. You're only doing it to irritate me.

RUSSELL: Am I?

MELANIE: Oh, do stop it.

RUSSELL: You know, I hadn't realised how sexy you are. You look to me as if you enjoy it. (*She looks as though she might slap his face. Or not.*) Well, I shall be finding out soon enough – shan't I? (*But she decides to play it cool.*)

MELANIE: And you – you enjoy it, I suppose?

RUSSELL: Oh, yes. I'm not bad at it either.

MELANIE: You surprise me.

RUSSELL: I dare say that's the Bamberg in me.

MELANIE: I dare say. (*Suddenly lost.*) Well –

RUSSELL: I think I'm going to enjoy this job.

MELANIE: (*Recovering.*) You're a cheap little man, aren't you?

RUSSELL: Yes. Very. But I'm all you've got.

MELANIE: I don't think you have any, any idea of what you're in for.

RUSSELL: I've been making enquiries. And seeing
you's clinched it.

MELANIE: Don't try to be gracious. It's
a little pathetic.

RUSSELL: I'm not being gracious. It's the truth.
Being alone with you in this soft, grey light,
being so close to you, I suddenly understand the
meaning of royalty. I feel the long, thrusting,
stimulus of the crown.

(*For a few moments they simply look at each other in the
cool light.*)

MELANIE: (*Softly.*) Do you know what to do?

RUSSELL: I think so.

MELANIE: I mean – during the ceremony.

RUSSELL: I'll manage.

MELANIE: I tell you: you don't know – you
simply don't know what you're letting yourself
in for. You've no idea of what it's like.

RUSSELL: I'll risk it.

MELANIE: You'll be like a badly trained poodle
going through its odious little tricks for the rest
of your life.

RUSSELL: I told you: you've sold me on it.

MELANIE: But you don't know what it's like.
Some days your head will start to spin
with boredom.

RUSSELL: Like yours.

MELANIE: Like mine. But I'm used to it. I've
been trained to it. But you – you'll crumble and
disintegrate with boredom. Your blood will rush
with constant hot and cold running boredom.

RUSSELL: Do you know: there's still a little spark
of life left somewhere there in you. I can see it,
I can actually see it now. Somewhere, there's
a little blundering glimmer of life left in you.

MELANIE: My whole weary system is spinning
around forever like a royal satellite in a space of
infinite and enduring boredom. Oh, my God, I am
so bored! (*She goes to the window.*) I am so bored,

do you hear me, my people? My countrymen,
I am so bored, and most of all, I am bored with
you, my people, my loyal subjects, I am so bored
that even this cheap little Australian looks like
relieving it for a few, brief moments, now and
then, in the rest of my lifetime.

RUSSELL: Just a few moments.

MELANIE: Very well.

(*They gaze at each other again.*)

RUSSELL: (*Presently.*) Looks like we've got a deal.

MELANIE: Yes. (*Pause.*) Do you want to kiss me?

(*He does so. She begins struggling, and pushes him away so
that he falls to the floor. She looks disturbed and frightened.*)
I can't bear to be touched!

(*She goes out. Enter TAFT.*)

RUSSELL: See you in church.

Scene 2

*The Cathedral. Fanfares. Salute of guns. Pealing bells. Choir of
splendid voices. All the massed devices of a Bamberg occasion, in fact.*

*MELANIE and RUSSELL are kneeling before the altar and about
to get up and begin their slow procession. Standing solemnly in the
front choir stalls are the BAMBERG FAMILY.*

*Downstage, WIMPLE and five other journalists are poised, waiting
to describe the scene. WIMPLE we know. The 1ST JOURNALIST is
a weary, solemn fellow from a weary, solemn newspaper. The 2ND
JOURNALIST is a bright, eager lady from a retarded glossy. The 3RD
JOURNALIST is from a right, rasping popular daily. The 4TH
JOURNALIST (lady or gentleman, it doesn't matter) is from a mass
woman's weekly. The 5TH JOURNALIST is the correspondent of
a large American News Agency.*

*TAFT and WITHERS stand to attention in full dress uniform nearby.
But before WIMPLE can start wimpling, the ARCHBISHOP speaks
before the altar.*

ARCHBISHOP: Lord, make us instruments of Thy
will; where there is hate, may we bring love;

where there is offence, may we bring pardon;
where there is discord, may we bring peace;
where there is error, may we bring truth; where
there is doubt, may we bring faith; where there
is despair, may we bring hope; where there is
darkness, may we bring light; where there is
sadness, may we bring joy. O Master, make us
seek not so much to be consoled as to console;
to be understood as to understand; to be loved
as to love. For it is in giving that we receive; in
self-forgetfulness that we find; in pardoning that
we are pardoned; in dying that we shall wake to
life eternal; where Thou livest and reignest in
the glory of the blessed Trinity, one God, world
without end.

WIMPLE: (*Scarcely breathing.*) Now – as the royal
couple, still kneeling on their faldstools, bow
their heads before the Archbishop, the choir and
congregation sing the cheerful and intensely
singable hymn, personally chosen by the couple
themselves, "O Perfect Love". In just a moment,
with the final triumphant fanfare, sounded by
trumpeters from the Prince's own regiment, the
Royal Bamberger Blues, you will see the Prince
and his bride slowly move along the aisle to the
Great West Door. My goodness, what a uniquely
impressive sight it all is! The Gentlemen-at-Arms
are there – you can probably see them – impassive
as always, the plumes of their helmets moving –
just ever so slightly in the merest current of
occasional air. If this were to be the end of all,
I think we could bravely – yes, bravely – say that
it was a good and a glorious end. Over there, on
the right, and next to His Majesty, is the young
Prince Heinrich, looking more confident than
when we saw him last on a similar occasion, the
wedding of his aunt last year. A fine, handsome
young man in his uniform, looking as cool as –
as a cucumber. From left to right, you can see,

or should be able to see, Princess Mariana, Duke George Stettin-Bamberg, the head of the Stettin-Bambergs, Princess Theresa, the Grand Duchess Isabella, Her Majesty the Queen, the young Prince Henry, His Majesty the King – Ah – now, they are, yes, they are beginning to rise – oh, what a moment, what a moment as the bride's train fans out in a fantastic, iridescent light, her veil, a superb cloud of zephyr-light silk tulle floats away there effortlessly, right there to the full extent of her exquisite train. Oh, oh, it's quite unbelievable in its solemn beauty, this moment – In loose formation, behind her, walk the pages and bridesmaids – including Princess Mariana – Now – Princess Melanie is indeed one of the family, and, as her handsome soldier husband leads her down the aisle, her royal cousins look on approvingly. What a sight it is! What a happy day for everyone! Only a very crabbed and gloomy heart could look on at this superb and moving spectacle without pride in his bosom and a catch at the back of his throat.

(*WIMPLE has a discreet catch at the back of his throat, while the other JOURNALISTS take over.*)

1ST JOURNALIST: It is all extremely picturesque, in the highest Bamberg tradition, measured and somewhat reminiscent of a Fackeltantz, which, it may be recalled, is a dance with torches in which only members of the blood royal may take part.

2ND JOURNALIST: The King looks especially handsome today in the full dress ceremonial uniform of the Twelfth Bamberg Lancers, with full decorations, of course –

3RD JOURNALIST: As one looked at her, the joy seemed almost too much for her slender figure to contain. But, as she was about to leave the altar, her face flew asunder in a great, glowing smile of simple, unaffected happiness.

4ᵀᴴ JOURNALIST: Beautiful wasn't the word for this bride. She was perfection. Against the greatest competition in the world, she moved like the right, royal lady she is. Like some serene swan, she floated rather than walked, down the aisle with her handsome soldier husband, towards her place in history.

5ᵀᴴ JOURNALIST: It is perhaps difficult for Americans to fully comprehend the strange, remote, religious element of majesty in these high European occasions. However, there is certainly no denying the extraordinary appeal of it, and ever since the first royal limousine, with its transparent hood, set out on the route, there has been fantastic frenzy here, in this ancient city that makes a New York City ticker-tape parade look like a high town carnival. No-one yet knows the number of men, women and children trampled to death in the mass enthusiasm, or even those who have perished from exposure. However, it is believed that the figures are considerable, and the casualty stations – socialised, of course – have been working at top pressure for hours.
(*The swelling volume of majestic sound and sense of hysteria becomes more and more intense and claustrophobic. The JOURNALISTS have to raise their voices a little, but they rasp on mechanically, lifelessly.*)

1ˢᵀ JOURNALIST: The Royal Wedding unites two families which both trace their ancestry in direct succession to King Stephen the First. Prince Wilhelm shares with Princess Melanie a
great great great
great great great
great great great
great great great
great great great
great great great
great-grandfather. However, in the case of the Princess, the number is one less.

2ND JOURNALIST: The Queen, lovely as always, is wearing a Marshall Waters powder blue ribbed satin outfit, with St Cyr hat in lilac organza. (*The PRINCE and PRINCESS are making their way down the aisle to the front of the stage.*)

1ST JOURNALIST: Happy is that land where the desire for symbols and display is expressed so harmlessly and yet so richly. Truly, an orb in the minster is worth a monster in orbit.

3RD JOURNALIST: To see this proud, fragile, yet superb rose of womanhood is almost too much for description. One can only try. Humbly and thankfully.

2ND JOURNALIST: Princess Theresa, always a treasure in pale colours, is wearing a frost-like satin outfit made by Percy Cummins –

4TH JOURNALIST: I think this has been the most romantic Royal Wedding of them all. Once or twice, the Prince seemed nervous and unsure of his lines, even fumbling some of the time-honoured gestures. But the Princess, by his side, quietly helped him through, and the few hold-ups that there were seemed scarcely noticeable –

2ND JOURNALIST: The Grand Duchess Isabella is wearing a Cummins champagne-coloured silk organdie outfit, embroidered with gold, diamante and topaz.

5TH JOURNALIST: It may be mysterious, incomprehensible but it's moving, certainly most important of all, it's moving. And a vindication of the Western Way of Life, against the threat of the Communist world. In all of this, my friends, our bastion lies.

4TH JOURNALIST: Yes, I think the moment I shall cherish most of all from this thrilling day is when the Princess looked up at her soldier husband, and smiled reassuringly at him, during the solemn service. It was an unforgettable moment, and, do you know, from where I was sitting, I suddenly saw her radiant young face look up into his and – yes – she *WINKED*.

2ND JOURNALIST: Isabella is in deep azalea organdie, fashioned by the House of Clough –

4TH JOURNALIST: She winked –

(*RUSSELL and MELANIE stop downstage.*)

RUSSELL: (*Smiling royally.*) I should have brought my camera.

MELANIE: No more pictures!

TAFT: (*To WITHERS.*) He's a Bamberg all right.

WIMPLE: And now, ladies and gentlemen, our National Anthem!

(*ALL stand to attention.*)

CHOIR: Long live the Bambergs
God Save Our Noble House
Long Live the Bambergs
Bless Our Noble House
Our Loving Prince and Princess
Our Kings and Noble Queens –
Long live our God-like – Kings and Queens!

The End.

UNDER PLAIN COVER

a play in one act

Characters

TIM

JENNY

POSTMAN

STANLEY

WEDDING GUESTS

REPORTERS

Under Plain Cover was first performed at the Royal Court Theatre, London, on 19 July 1962, by the English Stage Company. It was directed by Jonathan Miller, and the décor was by Alan Tagg. The cast was as follows:

TIM, Anton Rodgers

JENNY, Ann Beach

POSTMAN, Billy Russell

STANLEY, Glyn Owen

The outline of a house. Facing the audience a front door. Then, centre stage, a living room leading on to a bedroom. Beyond that a small room. All that can be seen of the bedroom is the bed, or part of it, through the partially open door.

In the living room there stands a dressmakers' dummy. A surgical trolley, a green screen, a couch, some sheets and blankets.

A POSTMAN carrying several parcels comes to the front door and rings the bell. From behind the screen a young man appears. He is dressed in a white coat with a stethoscope round his neck. He is pulling his trousers on. His name is TIM. He calls to the bedroom.

TIM: Will you go, or shall I?
  (*A girl's voice answers. It is JENNY.*)
JENNY: You!
TIM: I don't think I can. I've still got all this stuff on.
JENNY: Well, take it off. Damn it – it's not a full
  dress uniform.
  (*Bell rings again.*)
TIM: Damn! Please – you go. I went last time.
JENNY: Well, I should think so. I could hardly
  have gone in the circumstances. (*Giggles.*)
  (*He laughs too.*)
TIM: No, I suppose you couldn't really. Well, I'm
  still clearing this stuff away. (*TIM goes to the
  bedroom.*) Be a good girl. Go on. You look alright.
  He won't notice. (*Wheels trolley into bedroom.*)
JENNY: What do you mean – he won't notice. He
  can hardly help notice! Anyway, *who'll* notice?
TIM: The postman, you idiot. Come on. He's going
  away. We'll miss him.
JENNY: The postman. Oh, good. Are you sure?
TIM: Of course! (*Concerned.*) Darling – please. He's
  going away.
  (*Takes blanket into bedroom.*)
JENNY: Oh, alright then – I don't know what
  he'll think.
TIM: It doesn't matter what he thinks. He probably
  won't even recognise you.

JENNY: Of course he'll recognise me, you fool!

TIM: Answer the door! (*He goes to the window and shouts out.*) Just a minute. Please, darling! (*JENNY appears. She is dressed as a housemaid.*)

JENNY: You don't think he'll think I'm the maid, do you?

TIM: (*Agonised, pushes her.*) Oh, never mind. Who cares! It might be for you.

JENNY: Oh, yes! It might come today. How marvellous.

TIM: Just a minute. (*He grabs the green screen and takes it into the bedroom.*)

JENNY: (*Calling out.*) Coming!

TIM: Alright. You know how prying people are. (*She nods and goes to the door.*)

JENNY: Good morning!

POSTMAN: (*Dryly.*) Thought you'd gone on your holidays.

JENNY: Sorry.

POSTMAN: One for you. One for Mr Turner. (*He gives her a receipt to sign.*)

JENNY: Here?

POSTMAN: Usual place. Like one long Christmas for you, isn't it?

JENNY: (*Coldly.*) Thank you.

POSTMAN: Well, if it weren't for people like you and Mr Turner I suppose there'd be no work for people like –

JENNY: No. Good morning.

POSTMAN: Cheerio! (*She closes the door, examines the parcels.*)

JENNY: Darling!

TIM: (*Off.*) Did he notice anything?

JENNY: They've come.

TIM: Oh good!

JENNY: I don't think so. He was a bit cheeky, that's all. He's not as nice as the other one. Well, he'll get nothing at Christmas.

TIM: He must have thought you were mad. Must
think I'm mad, too, to let you do it.
(*He enters from bedroom. He is dressed in striped trousers
and black jacket. He carries a copy of* Country Life *and*
The Lancet.)
That's them! Isn't that super!

JENNY: There's yours. Shall we open them now?

TIM: No, let's keep them for later.

JENNY: Oh, come on – I'm dying to open them.

TIM: Well, that's fine. All the better. It'll do you
good to wait.

JENNY: I don't want to wait. (*Starts to open parcel.*)

TIM: Well, you've got to.

JENNY: Why?

TIM: Because *I* say so.

JENNY: Pooh!
(*His manner slides into a silky, menacing, authoritative tone,
slightly upper class. She becomes pert, cheeky.*)

TIM: Hand me those parcels! (*Puts on glasses, turns
to JENNY.*)

JENNY: What for? (*She steps back, clutching parcels.*)

TIM: Never mind what for – just hand them to me,
and don't be impertinent.
(*She hands them to him. He crosses to the kitchen.*)

JENNY: What are you going to do with them?

TIM: They're going into the staff room.

JENNY: Boo! I want mine!

TIM: You'll have it alright. (*Enters from the kitchen.*)

JENNY: When?

TIM: Later.

JENNY: Want it now.

TIM: You'll get it now, but you'll get something else.

JENNY: What will I get?

TIM: Wait and see.

JENNY: What will I get?

TIM: No.

JENNY: Go on.

TIM: No. Get my tea and tomato sandwiches.

JENNY: Please.

TIM: You heard me.

JENNY: Please – sir.

TIM: That's better. Well, Jenny, when you've got my tea and tomato sandwiches, we may discuss your problems then.

JENNY: Now!

(*TIM takes off glasses.*)

TIM: (*Anxiously.*) I think you mean it.

JENNY: I do.

TIM: (*In more ordinary voice.*) Do you?

(*She nods smugly.*)

Aren't you tired?

(*She shakes her head.*)

Blimey – well, you're a stronger man than I am. I need a cup of tea first, after that last lot.

(*She moves towards the bedroom.*)

NO!

(*She faces him mockingly. He resumes character.*)

Jenny! If you do not serve tea in – precisely two minutes –

JENNY: But I can't.

TIM: You'll have to.

JENNY: But it's not possible.

TIM: Everything is possible.

JENNY: No – it isn't. That's what you always say.

TIM: (*Coaxing.*) And aren't I right?

JENNY: No.

TIM: Jenny, serve tea. At once!

JENNY: What happens if I don't?

TIM: Do you really want to know?

JENNY: Yes. I think so.

TIM: If you don't serve my tea and tomato sandwiches – and everything must be absolutely immaculate, mind. Just as if it were a really posh house and you had to do this every day.

JENNY: Every day!

TIM: *You* should complain! The whole thing must be beautifully done. *You* know.

JENNY: Oh!

TIM: What?

JENNY: I don't think there are any clean napkins!

TIM: (*Grimly.*) There'd better be.

JENNY: Oh dear!

TIM: Or there'll be trouble.

JENNY: What sort of trouble?

TIM: Big trouble.

JENNY: How big?

TIM: Enormous.

JENNY: Well, go on – how big is that?

TIM: More than you can cope with anyway,
    young lady.

JENNY: (*Mocking.*) Oh, you're frightening me
    to death.

TIM: Now then!

JENNY: Sir!

TIM: Any more talk like that and you could find
    yourself in serious trouble. And you don't want
    that, do you?

JENNY: Oh, no, sir.

TIM: That's right.

JENNY: I've always been a very careful girl, sir.

TIM: Not careful enough.

JENNY: What's that?

TIM: Don't say what's that to me, girl. What do
    you call me, when you address me?

JENNY: Sir.

TIM: And what do you do?
    (*She curtsies. Does it badly and giggles.*)

JENNY: That wasn't very good.

TIM: No, it wasn't. I'll let it pass this time, but
    watch it.

JENNY: Yes, sir.

TIM: Watch it, because I've got my eyes on you all
    the time.

JENNY: I know, sir.

TIM: Every little move you make. Every little tiny
    slip goes down as a mark against you.

JENNY: A mark, sir?

TIM: A black mark.

JENNY: Oh dear, sir. Have I got any black marks already?

TIM: You have.

JENNY: How many?

TIM: (*Smugly.*) Quite a few.

JENNY: But how many, sir?

TIM: You'll find out.

JENNY: But I want to know, sir.

TIM: (*Cruelly.*) Why?

JENNY: Well, if I don't know, I may get upset and worried about it, when I'm getting the tea ready, and –

TIM: Yes?

JENNY: I may not serve it properly.

TIM: (*With crushing coolness.*) Well, that's *your* little problem isn't it? Now, don't stand around here talking all day. Serve tea.

JENNY: Yes, sir. (*She crosses to the kitchen door.*)

TIM: My Lord.

JENNY: Yes, my Lord. Oh – are you a lord?

TIM: Yes, I think so. Let's try it and see.

JENNY: Alright. I don't think it's so good, though.

TIM: Why?

JENNY: I don't know. I don't think you look quite right in that.

TIM: Yes – maybe you're right. OK. Leave it as it was. (*Reverting to character.*) Go on then. You don't want your cards, do you?

JENNY: No, sir.

TIM: You don't want to be dismissed without a reference, do you? (*He crosses over to her.*)

JENNY: Oh no, sir.

TIM: Think how upset your family would be if you lost your job. What would your father do to you?

JENNY: Take off his strap to me, sir.

TIM: Yes. There are plenty of girls just waiting, longing to step into your shoes.

JENNY: Yes, sir. Oh – is this the 1930s?

TIM: Yes.

JENNY: When did you think of that?

TIM: When do you think? Just now.

JENNY: Oh, what a good idea! Oh, please, sir. I need the job badly. Dad's still on the dole, and both me brothers are down bad.

TIM: Well, then – you'd better watch your behaviour, hadn't you?

JENNY: Yes, sir. I will. I'll do anything you say, sir – anything.

TIM: Very well then.

JENNY: Just give me a chance, then.

TIM: Now don't get hysterical, my dear. You'll be alright so long as you do exactly as you're told.

JENNY: Really, sir?

(*He nods, benignly.*)

Then I can stay, sir?

TIM: For the moment, Jenny, you may stay. And if I am satisfied with you, you may have no fears.

JENNY: Oh, thank you, sir.

TIM: That's enough. Tea, Jenny!

JENNY: Yes, sir. At once, sir. (*Goes into the kitchen.*)

TIM: Quickly, quickly! (*Sits.*)

JENNY: Oh, I'll try and not make any mistakes, sir. I'll do everything just as you like it, sir.

TIM: Alright, but I'll be watching you, Jenny. Remember, I'll be watching you.

(*He goes and sits down to read* Country Life. *She goes to the kitchen unit. Presently.*)

I'm waiting. (*Pause.*) I am waiting for my tea! (*Bawls.*) JENNY!

JENNY: The bell!

TIM: What? Oh, yes. Ding-a-ling!

(*He rings a sash bell. JENNY "appears" from the kitchen.*)

JENNY: Yes, sir?

TIM: The tea, Jenny. Where is the tea?

JENNY: I'm sorry, sir.

TIM: Don't stand there saying you're sorry.

JENNY: I'm sorry, sir.

TIM: Oh, for heaven's sake, girl, don't whine.
I can't stand it. What's the delay? Um?

JENNY: Well, I've got to wait for the water to boil.

TIM: Wait for the – ! Jenny, are you being
impertinent?

JENNY: No, sir – I –

TIM: I asked you a question: are you being
impertinent?

JENNY: I'm sorry, sir. I'm not feeling very well.

TIM: I've told you: don't snivel. You make me sick,
people like you. Do you think someone like me
is interested in your squalid little problems?

JENNY: No, sir – only –

TIM: Now, what is it. I warn you, Jenny. I am
really beginning to lose my temper.

JENNY: Oh, no –

TIM: And you know what that's likely to mean,
don't you?

JENNY: Oh, no – please, sir!

TIM: Well – you haven't much time.

JENNY: Excuse me, sir – the kettle's boiling, sir.
(*Goes to make tea.*)

TIM: (*Quietly.*) My patience is beginning to run out.

JENNY: Coming, sir! Just a few minutes.

TIM: Too long!

JENNY: What's that, sir?

TIM: I say too long. A few minutes is too long for
a man like me. One minute.

JENNY: Oh, sir –

TIM: One minute.

JENNY: Two minutes, sir. You'll have it in
two minutes.

TIM: One minute!

JENNY: One minute!

TIM: One minute!

JENNY: Make it two, please, sir.

TIM: One.

JENNY: It isn't long enough.

TIM: It's all you've got.

JENNY: Oh! (*Wails.*) How long have I got now, sir?

TIM: One minute, beginning now –

JENNY: Just a minute! (*JENNY enters.*)

TIM: What?

JENNY: Where's the flipping tea trolley?

TIM: In the bloody bedroom – where else?

JENNY: Oh, sorry. (*Goes into bedroom.*)

TIM: Twit. A right bloody housemaid you'd make.

JENNY: Alright, don't go raving mad. I forgot.
   (*Enters with trolley.*)

TIM: Yes, you forgot, didn't you! You forget too
   bloody much. Just you wait. One minute –
   from now.

JENNY: (*Cheeky, her identity poised.*) Well, you do
   look cross.

TIM: Ten – (*He paces left and right. JENNY lays trolley.*)

JENNY: You don't look very grand and sophisticated,
   do you?

TIM: Twenty –

JENNY: If I were a housemaid –

TIM: *What* did you say?

JENNY: Sorry. Well, you didn't look as though
   you'd command much respect from a dumb little
   tart like me.

TIM: Thirty –

JENNY: Oh, that's better. I say, you look quite
   terrifying now –

TIM: Forty –

JENNY: No, stop counting – that's not fair.

TIM: Forty-five –

JENNY: Oh, hell. I don't know what I've done with
   the bread and butter now.

TIM: Too bad. Just what I fancy today. Fifty –

JENNY: Oh, dear. Oh, there it is.

TIM: Brown, of course.

JENNY: Phew! Thank God I remembered.

TIM: And some white. Fifty-five.

JENNY: White! (*She grabs some and puts it on the trolley.*)

TIM: I hope you haven't forgotten anything. Sixty! You know how important my tea is to me. If I don't have it just as I like it, exactly as I think about it, it makes me unhappy, and I feel lost and lonely. You're 10 seconds late. And then I get vicious because even the tiny indispensable comforts of life are being denied me. And I need comfort, I need the comfort of home-made jam. Apricot jam. Twenty seconds late.

JENNY: No!

TIM: Blackcurrant jam and rhubarb jam that my father used to eat when he was a boy, and I've never been able to find or persuade anyone to make. Thirty seconds.

JENNY: It's here! It's here, sir. Here it is, sir. Your tea, sir.

TIM: And bloater paste and hot buttered toast. And gentleman's relish. Forty seconds.

JENNY: No – not forty seconds! It's here. Tea is served, sir.

TIM: And radishes! Hard and crisp and sparkling. Where are the radishes?

JENNY: On the little plate, sir.

TIM: Where?

JENNY: There, sir.

TIM: They don't look like the kind of radishes I always used to have. They're frozen radishes.

JENNY: No, sir.

TIM: How dare you, miss.

JENNY: No, sir – picked out of the garden, sir.

TIM: Frozen radishes! Fro – Radishes!

JENNY: No, fresh, sir.

TIM: Don't lie to me. You were one minute late in serving tea.

JENNY: No, sir – not one minute.

TIM: One minute!

JENNY: Forty seconds, sir.

TIM: Fifty seconds.

JENNY: Forty, sir.

TIM: Fifty.

(*She is about to argue. But he grabs her hair.*)

Ah! Now then, do you know what happens to naughty little housemaids who bring me my tea late.

JENNY: No, sir.

TIM: Don't you?

JENNY: No, sir.

TIM: Well, for every 10 seconds that they're late –

JENNY: Every 10 seconds!

TIM: Every 10 seconds.

JENNY: It was 30 last time.

TIM: Never mind. It's 10 now. You've been very naughty.

JENNY: Well, it's not fair. (*Rams him with her head.*)

TIM: Of course, it isn't fair. As I was saying, for every 10 seconds that you are late, you will be very severely punished. (*Kisses her.*)

JENNY: Every 10. That's four.

TIM: Five. Very severely indeed.

JENNY: You seem to make up all the rules. (*TIM lets go her hair.*)

TIM: Naturally. That is what I was born to.

JENNY: Well, I think I'll give in my notice.

TIM: You can't.

JENNY: My dad'll understand – especially when I tell him the kind of man you are. I'll get another job.

TIM: It's the 1930s.

JENNY: Oh yes, I forgot that.

TIM: Well, you haven't much choice, have you?

JENNY: I suppose I haven't.

TIM: Speak up. And pour me my tea. (*Sits.*)

JENNY: Yes, sir. (*Goes to trolley.*)

TIM: In addition to this other punishment, you have a considerable number of black marks against you.

JENNY: Oh! Have I? Many?

TIM: About a dozen.

JENNY: A dozen! There can't be.

TIM: You've just put sugar in my tea. That's 13.

JENNY: Oh!

TIM: There's no jam spoon, 14; cake knife, 15, and I can see a slug on the watercress – *two* black marks for that! That's 17 altogether, and I've hardly begun.

JENNY: Oh, sir, it's too much!

TIM: Whose fault is that?

JENNY: I'll try, sir, honestly I will!

TIM: You should have thought of that before, shouldn't you!

JENNY: I don't think I can bear it!

TIM: You've got to.

JENNY: Have a little mercy, sir.

TIM: You must learn to take your punishment properly.

JENNY: I'm an ignorant girl, sir!

TIM: So much the better!

(*She starts snivelling.*)

Stop that! You'll have something to snivel for later. Go and wait for me.

JENNY: No, sir.

TIM: JENNY!

JENNY: Very good, sir. (*Goes to the door and leans on it.*)

TIM: Well, what are you waiting for?

JENNY: How many did you say, sir?

TIM: Seventeen.

JENNY: Seventeen!

TIM: Plus five.

JENNY: Plus five. Oh – I'd forgotten that.

TIM: Yes. I thought you might have. Get along then.

JENNY: How long will you be?

TIM: Sir?

JENNY: Sir.

TIM: I don't know how long I shall be, Jenny.
I shall see. But I shall certainly finish my tea first.

JENNY: But you don't know what it's like to wait!

TIM: I – don't know – what it's like – TO WAIT!

JENNY: Forgive me.

TIM: You shall wait even longer. Just for that.

JENNY: Well, not too long then, because I'm –

TIM: You've already got 17 plus five. You don't
want any more, do you?

JENNY: I've gone.

*(She disappears into the bedroom. He settles down rather
agitated to his tea.)*

TIM: Ugh! You do make a lousy cup of tea.

JENNY: *(Off.)* What's that?

TIM: I'm damned glad I don't employ you,
that's all.

JENNY: Can't hear you.

(Pause. He eats.)

TIM: No tomato sandwiches.

JENNY: What you say?

TIM: No tomato sandwiches.

JENNY: Oh, my God! I forgot.

TIM: You forgot alright. Well, you're in dead
trouble now! *(He munches over* Country Life.*)*

JENNY: *(Off.)* I'm ready.

(He ignores her.)

I said – yoo hoo! I'm ready!

TIM: What is that to me, girl? Domestic servants do
not shout through open doors at their masters.

JENNY: Please – I'm sorry, sir.

TIM: No excuses. That's even more trouble.

JENNY: No.

(Pause.)

Please. I'm exhausted.

87

TIM: Well, that's just too bad. You bloody wait!

JENNY: (*Off.*) What?

TIM: I said you bloody wait, you horrible
    little skivvy!

JENNY: Oh!
    (*Whimper off.*)

TIM: (*Settling down.*) I'm having my tea.
                    (*Fade.*)

*Downstage a reporter, STANLEY, appears. He is middle-aged and
the worse for wear.*

STANLEY: Just an ordinary, young married couple
    you might think. A lot of people are inclined to
    sneer at us, but in my job you do get to know
    quite a bit about human nature and what makes
    people tick. Their hopes, and fears, their little
    ambitions. Take this couple for instance: not
    long married, not too well off, but doing quite
    nicely, both working till they decide to start
    a family. Like a million others. Or, at least,
    that's what they thought. That's what you would
    have thought – ordinary members of the public.
    That's what I would have thought.
    (*The POSTMAN crosses to the front door.*)
    Excuse me –

POSTMAN: Yes?

STANLEY: Are you delivering that at this house?

POSTMAN: I am.

STANLEY: Mr and Mrs Turner, isn't it?

POSTMAN: That's right. What do you want?

STANLEY: What sort of couple are they?

POSTMAN: Just an ordinary couple. Here, you're
    Press, aren't you?

STANLEY: Don't tell me *you've* got a grudge.
    We did you boys rather well over your wage
    demand, didn't we?

POSTMAN: (*Dryly.*) Thanks, mate. You can carry
    me sack for me, too, if you like.

(*STANLEY goes out to right assembly. Goes to door, rings, whistles. Lights up in house. TIM is reading the mail order advertisements in a pile of newspapers. Occasionally he marks one. He is dressed as a boxer in bright shorts, dressing gown, boots and gloves. Over by the screen is a milliner's dummy wearing a corset.*)

TIM: Darling!

JENNY: (*Off.*) If you mean the doorbell, I'm not answering it.

TIM: Why not?

JENNY: Don't be so dim!

TIM: Well, I can't go. He'll go away again. Oh, do go! (*TIM rises, crosses to chair and sits. JENNY appears. She is dressed as a Girl Guide.*)

JENNY: I can't go like this.

TIM: Yes, you can.

JENNY: Well, I won't.

TIM: You can pretend you're someone else. That hat just about covers your face.

JENNY: Go on!

TIM: How can I go? With these. (*Lifts his gloves.*) I can't even open the doorhandle. I'm helpless.

JENNY: I'll say you are! Oh, alright then. They can wait a minute. (*TIM puts the dummy behind the screen.*)

TIM: (*Calls out.*) Coming! (*He nods to her and sits down. JENNY opens the door.*)

JENNY: Good morning!

POSTMAN: Thought you'd fallen down the hole.

JENNY: What hole?

POSTMAN: Never mind! One for Mrs Turner. (*He gives her the receipt to sign.*)

JENNY: Here?

POSTMAN: That's right. Mrs Turner away?

JENNY: Yes.

POSTMAN: Who are you? You're the little sister, I suppose.

JENNY: That's right. Nothing for Mr Turner?

POSTMAN: No. That's all this time.

TIM: Oh, *hell!*

POSTMAN: Cheerio then!

JENNY: 'Bye! (*She closes the door. Puts parcel on the floor.*) What a shame!

TIM: Damn! (*Sits.*)

JENNY: Never mind.

TIM: I'd been thinking about that all the morning.

JENNY: Perhaps it'll come this afternoon. Look – mine's come.

TIM: Well, that's something.

JENNY: Well, that's something. Don't be such a misery. Or I shan't open it. (*She goes into the bedroom.*)

TIM: Where are you going?

JENNY: (*Off.*) To take these off.

TIM: Oh! Aren't you going to open it?

JENNY: I don't know.

TIM: What do you mean, you don't know?
(*JENNY appears at the door, taking off her tunic.*)

JENNY: Depends how you are.

TIM: Here, help me off with these gloves, will you?

JENNY: (*Going into bedroom.*) Hang on for a bit, I want to hang this up before it gets creased any more.

TIM: Whose fault is that?

JENNY: I don't know what you mean. I feel rather good today.

TIM: Yes. I think I do too. I liked this morning.

JENNY: Well – (*Parody.*) – it's something different.

TIM: Yes. Makes a change.

JENNY: Bit more out of the usual run, like. What's in the papers?

TIM: I haven't had a chance yet. I wish you'd help me with these gloves. I'm breaking my teeth on these strings.

JENNY: Don't be so impatient. (*TIM starts to read paper on table.*)

TIM: Hey, what are champers?

JENNY: What are what?

TIM: Champers.

JENNY: Spell it!

TIM: C-H-A-M-P-E-R-S.

JENNY: Never heard of them.

TIM: Oh – I see!

JENNY: They sound a bit exotic.

TIM: It's alright. It's champagne.

JENNY: You fool!

TIM: It's the way I read it. Only it looked a bit
     sort of medieval in the context. Like he died of
     a surfeit of champers. Did I tell you about the
     Champagne Queen?

JENNY: No – what?

TIM: He likes to get his boyfriend's slipper –
     and drink –

JENNY: Don't tell me –

TIM: And then there's the Jesus Queen.

JENNY: What's he do?

TIM: Likes to be crucified. Oh yes, and then
     there's the Jessie Mathews Queen.

JENNY: What about her?

TIM: She dances overhead, on the ceiling, on my
     bed! Help me!

JENNY: Coming! (*She comes in wearing a dressing gown,
     helps him off with his gloves.*)

TIM: And then we can look at your parcel.

JENNY: Papers first.

TIM: Usual stuff, I think.

JENNY: Never mind. We don't want to miss anything.

TIM: There's a picture of George and Betty's
     wedding in the local.

JENNY: Oh, where? Let me see.
     (*Shows her.*)
     They look nice. I'm crazy about that dress. Why
     don't we get one?

TIM: What a smashing idea. Where?

JENNY: I don't know. Expensive item. That's why
we got married in a registry office, remember?

TIM: When? When can we have –

JENNY: You be a good boy. And we'll see.

TIM: Jenny – (*He kisses her.*)

JENNY: Yes?

TIM: Please can we have a wedding dress
like Betty's?

JENNY: We'll see.

TIM: Perhaps we could have Betty's. People don't
want wedding dresses after they're married.

JENNY: We'll see.

TIM: Oh, you sound like my bloody aunt.

JENNY: I'll give you a good smack in a minute.

TIM: You didn't say that when I had the gloves on.

JENNY: Looks a super wedding. Wish we'd gone.

TIM: Well, I don't.

JENNY: I think we ought to go out sometimes.

TIM: You don't really want to go out, do you?

JENNY: No, not really. Only –

TIM: Only what?

JENNY: No, you're right. I don't really want to either.
Anyway, you'd have had to be the best man.

TIM: I thought of that. Might have felt a bit funny,
standing up there at the altar. You know – when
you've been on intimate terms with the bride
and the groom. Who's that?

JENNY: Which?

TIM: The bridesmaid – second from the right.

JENNY: That? Oh, you know who that is –
that's Brenda.

TIM: Brenda –

JENNY: Brenda Rose.

TIM: Brenda Rose. Of course, I remember her –
years ago. Tall.

JENNY: That's right.

TIM: I remember her very well. She had very
fair-coloured hair, and deep blue knickers.

JENNY: That reminds me –

TIM: What?

JENNY: Papers.

TIM: Alright. Papers. Then parcel. Right?

JENNY: OK.

(*They settle down happily, seriously.*)

TIM: She was a funny girl.

JENNY: Who?

TIM: Betty.

JENNY: Oh!

TIM: Rather toffee-nosed sort of girl. Always used to take her dog with her to parties so that she could talk to it – just to show how bored she was.

JENNY: Sounds sweet. Here, is this the same as ours? (*Hands him paper.*)
(*Reading.*) Adjustable Dress Dummy. In tough plastic. Thirty-eight shillings.

TIM: How much was ours?

JENNY: You know, I can't remember.

TIM: (*Reading.*) Fully finished set of parts which clip together and adjust to size and height. Can grow and change with you.

JENNY: Oh, yes, that must be it.

TIM: (*Reading.*) No skill, tools or extras required. Money back guarantee.

JENNY: Well, I wouldn't mind having ours back.

TIM: No, it was a bit of a washout, that, wasn't it?

JENNY: Hey, do men get a funny feeling when they do their coat buttons up?

TIM: What – overcoat?

JENNY: Well – yes.

TIM: Don't know. Can't say I've noticed it. Why? Do you?

JENNY: Yes.

TIM: How interesting. Do all women?

JENNY: Shouldn't think so.

TIM: You've never mentioned that before.

JENNY: I suddenly realised it yesterday morning when I took my coat off at the office. I thought of you.

TIM: Darling. (*Reading.*) Wendle's Specialist
    Commode five pounds twelve and six.

JENNY: That's always in.

TIM: (*Reading.*) Made by craftsmen with real oak
    finish. Upholstered seat covered with green
    simulated leather. Deluxe model with
    Dunlopillo.

JENNY: Oh, deluxe, I think.

TIM: Yes, I think it's worth extra. (*Reading.*)
    Upholstered seat in red, blue or beige moquette.
    Hygienic pan with handle.

JENNY: I've got one here for only four pounds
    ten, delightfully discreet. In woven fibre and
    pastel shades of lilac, rose, or blue – or all gold
    finish. This has a hygienic polythene pan. Can't
    you forget your rupture?

TIM: Don't.

JENNY: This is the modern method of control,
    gentle, natural, easy.

TIM: It will enable you to carry on your normal
    pursuits, however strenuous, without
    understraps, hip pressure or chafing.

JENNY: You can experience for the first time
    a real feeling of elation.

TIM: There's a plastic object here.

JENNY: Varicose veins –

TIM: As used by the Convent of St Bridget in
    Limerick. It has a little battery in it that
    lights up.

JENNY: Flatten that bulge and improve your
    figure with this amazing belt.

TIM: What's that?

JENNY: Not a pull-on. Elastic sides.

TIM: Ah!

JENNY: Fitted with suspenders and adjustable
    understraps. State size round middle of stomach.
    Also anti-stoop braces.

TIM: Well, there's something in that –

JENNY: Something in what?

TIM: Something in that, as the monkey said, as he scratched his head –

JENNY: What?

TIM: In the night commode.

JENNY: Maternity fashions.

TIM: Oh, yes – read those. (*Rises into squatting position facing her.*)

JENNY: Thought that would rouse you. Um – oh, it's not very interesting.

TIM: Come on. Read it out.

JENNY: No really. It's just rather dull, really – Nothing for us.

TIM: I wish you wouldn't keep staring at my hairline.

JENNY: Was I?

TIM: Yes, you make me feel I've got dandruff.

JENNY: Sorry.

TIM: Well, don't look away like that. You've been transfixed above my eyeline for 10 minutes.

JENNY: I haven't.

TIM: Well, have I?

JENNY: What?

TIM: Got dandruff?

JENNY: Oh, don't be so silly –

TIM: Have I?

JENNY: Yes.

TIM: Oh, God, I knew it! Damn you! (*Goes to mirror.*)

JENNY: New, unissued US Air Force Officers' vests and fronts. Specially designed for the British climate. Pure wool for warmth and interwoven with white rayon on inner side to prevent irritation.

TIM: Damn! So I have!

JENNY: For the man who dare not take risks. Oh, come on! Hygienic sanitation without mains, flushit. Fully flushing. No emptying by hand. Fully automatic. *C'est magnifique.*

TIM: What is?

JENNY: French rubber gloves.

TIM: Oh, yes? Really? What's that?

JENNY: These fully fashioned supple glovelies.

TIM: Glovelies?

JENNY: Made by French designers with palms and fingers to give a superb grip. Delightfully feminine in ravishing pink.

TIM: Let's have a look.

JENNY: Foam-filled cushions. Four-way-strech non-iron snug-fit covers in sophisticated, mottled, elegant paisley, contemporary leaf and beautiful Jacobean designs.

TIM: Darling –

JENNY: Oh – there are those waders – thigh length – fully waterproof. Gosh! Yes?

TIM: Do you think I'm fixated?

JENNY: No – I don't think you are. Oh, there's a skull lamp for car or home – twenty-seven and six. Also as a TV lamp for the home. State model required. Guaranteed money back if not satisfied.

TIM: Are you sure?

JENNY: Yes. Why, you don't you think you are, do you?

TIM: No. I'm quite sure I'm not. I just wondered if you thought I was.

JENNY: No. I'd tell you if I thought so. Beautiful foam-filled bath head-rest. *Relaxez-vous.* Luring foam rubber interior. Plastic outer cover in pastel shades with floral or white lace effect. I think you're probably fixated.

TIM: Yes?

JENNY: New-type suction fitting attached to rear flap eliminates strain.

TIM: Well, you're probably right about that.

JENNY: Stick-o-Quilt. Glamorise your bed heads. Lace and nylon waist petticoats, two for nineteen and eleven.

TIM: Yes?

JENNY: Nine-inch nylon lace trimming and ruched panel. Pink, lilac, mimosa. No, I don't think so.

TIM: No bones about it – superb corselette.

JENNY: Size: W's only. That's unusual. Super sleeping-bags. Safe and comfortable. Wonder what they mean, safe. Nylon nighties: exciting, alluring in petal pink, blue, aqua and primrose.

TIM: Are they?

JENNY: Shorties – what?

TIM: Alluring?

JENNY: No. With cheeky bloomers.

TIM: What about these?

JENNY: Don't know. I'll mark them anyway.

TIM: Does it say anything else?

JENNY: Same price and colours. W and WX only. Pity they don't do SW.

TIM: I prefer W.

JENNY: I know, but with some things it's a little too large. These skirts look rather good.

TIM: Oh, yes. They look really common, don't they? Like the plastic car covers.

JENNY: With reinforced eyelets.

TIM: In deep grey, olive, mink, bottle, African violet, nigger, navy and black.

JENNY: Zip placket.

TIM: Double thickness polythene. Does not wobble or sag.

JENNY: Here we are. The French Riviera. Oxford. The Norfolk Broads.

TIM: Never before has such value been offered in napkins. Wonderful soft quality, these full-size napkins will wash and wear well, giving no cause for complaint. Do you think they mean table napkins or babies' napkins?

JENNY: Babies. Here it is.

TIM: Yes?

JENNY: Sensational value! Directoire knickers. Three pairs for fourteen and eleven. Hips 38 to 44.

TIM: Gosh, why do they make them so bloody big?

JENNY: Always the same. Three pairs for seventeen and eleven. Hips 46 to 54.

TIM: Forty-six to 54!

JENNY: Good night! Made in wonderful heavy quality interlock. Long leg –

TIM: Good!

JENNY: And wide gusset.

TIM: Gusset!

JENNY: Elasticated waist and legs. So comfortable. In blue, pink or green.

TIM: What else?

JENNY: Well, there's peach.

TIM: Of course.

JENNY: Champagne. And, of course, black and white. Bottle.

TIM: Nigger.

JENNY: Knickers for niggers.

TIM: Let's have some coffee. I feel tired.

JENNY: I'm not surprised. (*She goes to the kitchen unit.*) And then we'll open our parcel, shall we?

TIM: OK. (*Sings.*)
Knickers, knickers, these are the thing to 'ave,
You puts them on in the bedroom,
You takes them off in the lav –

JENNY: Are you alright?

TIM: Yes, I'm alright. (*Sings.*)
Knickers, knickers, these are the things to wear,
For if you buy a pair of knickers,
Then you won't have your bum all bare.
(*Speaks.*) Why? Don't I sound alright?

JENNY: No, you sound a bit depressed.

TIM: Oh, sorry.

JENNY: That's alright.

TIM: Well, I am a bit. Hey – do you think we're living on relics?

JENNY: Who?

TIM: You and me.

JENNY: Probably.

TIM: So do I. Do you think they're diminishing in some way?

JENNY: What? (*Goes to kitchen door.*)

TIM: Well, knickers, for instance.

JENNY: No, why should they be? (*Goes out.*)

TIM: You're sure?

JENNY: Quite. Why, aren't you?

TIM: (*Rises.*) I think so. I ask myself: *am I diminished?* But I can't always be sure.
(*JENNY at kitchen door.*)

JENNY: You brood too much. You should get out.

TIM: I don't want to get out. (*Sits.*)

JENNY: Alright. Well, maybe sometimes you should, anyway.

TIM: What do they represent, in particular?

JENNY: Take down your particulars.

TIM: Your step-ins.

JENNY: Your what?

TIM: I seem to remember that once. Your drawers, your taxi-teasers, your unmentionables. What do we know about them? Are they symbols then? In that case, not only do they convey ideas, but they do things. Saint Augustine once said that a handshake doesn't just express friendship. It promotes it. Your milk's boiling over.

JENNY: Damn! Go on! (*She rushes to milk.*)

TIM: Or is it straightforward and not really open to serious speculation? Like my hairdresser said about that new musical in London; no message, dear. Just lots of lovely people enjoying themselves. Do we demand an ethic of frankness? Or is it simply a matter of private faces in public places? But should the facts about recusant lingerie be made known? Are they to be pressed in old books and forgotten, instead of being tended as objects rooted in the deepest needs of the personality? Attention must be paid!

JENNY: Hear, hear!

TIM: Great love springs from great knowledge.

JENNY: We've got that –

TIM: This is the most challenging moral issue of our time.

JENNY: The choice between open ends and ETBs.

TIM: Elastic top and bottoms. Oh, I've just thought of another – the Judas Queen.

JENNY: What does she like?

TIM: Being picked up in a loo, and then betrayed to the police. Oh, you'll wonder where the fellow went, when they wash your brains in Pepsodent.

JENNY: Here's your coffee. You sound a bit better.

TIM: Just a little.

JENNY: Why don't you take off your dressing gown?

TIM: Why?

JENNY: You look hot.

TIM: I am hot. I've always been hot. When I was younger I was skinny and afraid to take my clothes off. Now I'm ashamed because I'm too fat.

JENNY: You're not too fat. I think you're just right.

TIM: Well – I'm 29. Not much time. Erasmus didn't start learning Greek till he was 34, you know. Still, there's a lot of difference between him and me. Oh, thou that tellest glad tidings to Zion, arise, shine, for thy light is come.

JENNY: Have you got sugar?

TIM: No – fattening. Get thee up into the high mountain! Why don't we have another baby?

JENNY: Why not?

TIM: That's good. I wonder if Erasmus wore knickers.

JENNY: He probably didn't think they were important – very significant.

TIM: Probably. You won't forget about getting that wedding dress, will you?

JENNY: No.

TIM: Promise?

JENNY: Promise.

TIM: Only if you get pregnant again, we shall need it.

JENNY: Don't worry. I'll get it.

TIM: Hey, you know that woman in the hospital.

JENNY: The Lady Almoner?

TIM: That's right – the one who –

JENNY: The one you say looks just like me.

TIM: Yes.

JENNY: Charming.

TIM: Give us a kiss.

JENNY: What about her?

TIM: Give us a kiss!

JENNY: Oh, alright.

TIM: Why don't you –

JENNY: Why don't I get an overall just like hers!

TIM: That's right. Well?

JENNY: I've already thought of it. We've been
    spending far too much lately, you know that.

TIM: Oh, come on – you look just like her.

JENNY: No!

TIM: Alright – you don't look like her.

JENNY: Well, we'll see.

TIM: What about her? The Lady Almoner?

JENNY: What – underwear?

TIM: Yes. Pretty meagre, I should think, wouldn't
    you? Sort of shrivelled, crabbed, paltry things.

JENNY: Oh, absolutely. Ungenerous. Nothing
    expensive or friendly or welcoming.

TIM: Exactly. Nothing comforting or reassuring.
    Oh, God: isn't it a mess!

JENNY: Yes.

TIM: The Vision of Knickers that thou dost see, is
    my Vision's Greatest Enemy.

JENNY: Who said that?

TIM: Blake.

JENNY: Yes, I thought it was. As a matter of fact,
    I can tell you exactly what they'd be like.

TIM: What?

JENNY: The Lady Almoner's.

TIM: Oh yes?

JENNY: Well, in the first place, white, I should say.

TIM: Oh yes – white definitely.

JENNY: Upper class colour – they nearly always wear white. With a slip always. And the satin ribbon a little too loose. Pants with what are called French ends – open ends in the trade. Er. Wearing *cornet du bal*.

TIM: Yes. Absolutely. Perfect. I was wrong. You're not like her at all. (*Kisses dummy.*)

JENNY: Do you think there are many people like us?

TIM: No. Probably none at all, I expect.

JENNY: Oh, there must be some.

TIM: Well, yes, but probably not two together.

JENNY: You mean just one on their own?

TIM: Yes.

JENNY: How awful. We are lucky.

TIM: I know.

JENNY: What's the matter?

TIM: I don't know. I think I feel ill.

JENNY: In what way?

TIM: Every way. I'm always feeling ill, and there's nothing at all the matter with me. Isn't it boring. I wish I wasn't so boring. (*Throws dummy on to floor.*)

JENNY: You're not. (*Rises.*)

TIM: Well, I wish I wasn't feeling ill anyway.

JENNY: Still?

TIM: No. I'm slightly better. (*Picks up dummy, resets it.*)

JENNY: If I open the parcel – will that make you feel better?

TIM: I don't know. Wait for a few minutes. Maybe if I have another cup of coffee I'll feel better. I wanted to ask you something.

JENNY: Yes?

TIM: What was it? Oh, yes – I have an *idée fixe* –

JENNY: Oh, no you haven't. I wouldn't have one in the house.

TIM: Really. I know. Tell me, I want your definition.

JENNY: You don't remember it very well. I've explained it to you enough times.

TIM: Well, I like to hear you say it. Go on.

JENNY: Oh, alright –

TIM: Oh, just a minute – I've thought of something.

JENNY: Well?

TIM: The Prime Minister's Country House – seat: Knickers.

JENNY: Of course. Why don't you come down for the weekend?

TIM: Open to the public on weekdays.

JENNY: Until they pull it down. Well now –

TIM: Oh, yes – remind me to tell you something afterwards.

JENNY: Shall I begin?

TIM: Please. Oh, just while I remember: it is *interlock* we don't like, isn't it?

JENNY: Yes. Now. Shall I begin?

TIM: Sorry. Why did the lady with a wooden leg have no change for a pound?

JENNY: Oh, alright, if –

TIM: She only had a half a knicker. (*Kisses JENNY.*)

JENNY: (*Firmly.*) First of all – pants. To a specialist, one should remember that this is not the generic word. It means that they don't have elastic at the bottom.

TIM: Just left open to speculation.

JENNY: Exactly. The Americans have perverted this, and created a very loose generic word "panties". Now, briefs are what every girl wears nowadays.

TIM: Alas!

JENNY: Closed at the bottom of the leg, and leaving about four inches of girdle showing on the thigh. Then there are what are called bikini briefs.

TIM: And very nasty too!

JENNY: Which are the final sophistication of the brief form, and leave the navel showing as long

as you haven't a girdle on. And about, oh, six
to eight inches of flank. Finally we come to the
flower of the form, believed by most to be
decadent. They have long legs, never more
than about four inches above the knee, which
makes sitting down, getting out of cars, riding
bicycles or going upstairs in buses a tremendous
adventure. They always – repeat always – have
elastic top and bottom. What the flying buttress
was to Gothic so is elastic top and bottom to the
Classical Perpendicular or Directoire style. And
it is only in knickers that one is still able to find
that strange repository of mystery – the gusset.

TIM: Ah – the gusset – (*Pause.*) I wonder what that
chap Betjeman would say about all this.

JENNY: Nowadays they are mostly worn by
elderly or overly square middle-aged ladies, and
can still be bought in fast-decreasing numbers
from places like Debenham and Freebody,
although High Street Kensington still remains
the richest field, with Derry and Toms and, above
all, Pontings, stubbornly carrying on the old
tradition. I suppose one might almost say that the
end of the knickers came with the rise of nylon.

TIM: True. It was nylon really killed them.

JENNY: They were never quite the same afterwards.
The heavy whisper of descending pink silk was
soon to be heard in the land no more. All was
hard-faced, unembarrassed, unwelcoming nylon.
Of course, in their most basic form, they can still
be seen on schoolgirls trooping by the dozen into
their gymnasiums in drab navy. But only very
square little girls still really wear them long.

TIM: Yes, I remember them. Hundreds of them.
Sometimes they were dark green.

JENNY: Bottle.

TIM: But mostly navy. Still, even they were better
than nothing. (*Pause.*) They often had pockets in
them, didn't they?

JENNY: That's right. I used to keep my handkerchief or toffees in there.

TIM: Really? I once knew a girl who used to keep her sweet coupons in there. Then there were French knickers –

JENNY: And cami-knickers. They were very odd. I think my mother had them in her trousseau. It was really a truncated slip in what was known as art silk –

TIM: Like art cinema –

JENNY: It wasn't really silk at all. There was a tongue at the front and the back of the skirt which buttoned up in the crutch.

TIM: Or crotch as the case might be. What about bloomers?

JENNY: I suppose they were really the first dab at the form.

TIM: Mrs Bloomer, that's right.

JENNY: Then I seem to remember there was something called a lingerie set, in one-faced satin, which, I think, was dull on one side and shiny on the other.

TIM: I adore listening to you talk.

JENNY: No, wait a minute – I'm wrong. They were called a slip and knicker set. That's right. You'd say: my mother's bought me a slip and knicker set for Christmas.

TIM: You seem to know everything!

JENNY: Well, I'm going to open my parcel.

TIM: Oh, good.

JENNY: And you can change, too.

TIM: Yes, I'd better, hadn't I?

JENNY: Yes, you had, or you'll get into trouble, won't you? You look better after that.

TIM: Yes. I am. Thank you.

(*He goes to behind screen, to change. JENNY goes into the bedroom.*)

Oh, I know what I meant to tell you. When I was getting a postal order for that last lot, I thought of a collective name for them.

JENNY: (*Off.*) What, like a flock of knickers? Or a pride of knickers.

TIM: Oh, that's not bad either. Mine's a charisma of knickers.

JENNY: (*Off.*) Too fancy.

TIM: (*Disappointed.*) Oh!

JENNY: (*Off.*) Nobody knows what it means.

TIM: (*To himself.*) Knickers, the eponymous hero of the trilogy. Hey, what about the critics?

JENNY: (*Off.*) What about them?

TIM: Well, you know. This week, we have been to see *Knickers.* What did we feel about this? *Soaptender*: Well, in the first place, there seemed to me to be far too much production. And production of a kind I find particularly irksome. After all, we saw all this in the twenties surely. Expressionism and everything.

JENNY: (*Off.*) If only the verse could be allowed to speak for itself.

TIM: Exactly. (*He comes out dressed in winceyette pyjamas and heavy woollen dressing-gown.*) As for the garment itself. Well, construction is weak, of course. So is plot. But we have learned in recent years to bear with that somewhat in exchange for a little vitality. But somehow this elastic doesn't seem to know exactly what it's aimed at, and the final gesture is totally inadequate, irrelevant and with a basic failure to be coherent. We are left to work out our own causes. Futility is our only clue. (*Goes into bedroom and returns with a pile of knickers.*) It seems to me that these knickers are speaking out of a private, obsessional world – full of meaning for them. But has it any significance for us? I think not. On the whole, a dull, rather distasteful evening.

JENNY: (*Off.*) Not without quality. On the other hand, I would not say straight out it had no quality at all. What do the others think?

TIM: Doesn't seem to have found an entirely satisfactory form for what they are trying to say. The reason for the elastic is never clearly or adequately explained.

JENNY: (*Off.*) By no means a total artistic success.

TIM: (*Puts a pair on his head and stalks up and down.*) I thought them schoolgirlish and sniggering. Very tiresome indeed. At least bikinis are brief! It's all very vigorous in an undisciplined way. One does get so tired of these chips on the gusset. Very self indulgent and over-strident, especially in the length of leg, I thought. (*Takes knickers off head.*) Colour was reasonable, but surely Herbert Farjeon did these with much more taste and economy? And after all, this frenetic destructiveness is hardly helpful. What do they really offer to put up as an alternative? We are left unsatisfied with questions posed and nothing answered. Hear, hear! This sour soufflé certainly failed to rise for me. Although everyone tried hard enough. I suppose what they were aiming at was pure lingerie. Ah – you mean like pure cinema. Exactly, and then, of course, there's the obvious influence of Genet. Indeed. To say nothing of –

> James
> Ionesco
> Fanny Burney
> Troise

– and his mandoliers, too. Let's not forget them.

JENNY: (*Off.*) That influence is quite clear. How would you describe the style?

TIM: Style.

(*Throws knickers pair by pair on to the floor.*)

> Florid.
> Decadent.
> Unnecessary repetition.
> Neo-classical.

      Baroque.

      Kafkaesque.

      Fin de Siècle.

      Je M'en Fous.

      Arcane.

      Elliptical   Elastical.

JENNY: (*Off.*) So, how would you sum up, ladies and gentlemen?

TIM: (*Picks up knickers.*) Well, within their own terms, these knickers may seem to work, but what is the manufacturer's attitude to them?

JENNY: (*Off.*) What does "within their own terms these knickers may seem to work" mean?

TIM: It means you enjoyed yourself (*Throws knickers into bedroom.*) at the time, but now you're ashamed to admit it!

(*JENNY comes in dressed as a nurse in black stockings, standard cap and cuffs, etc. TIM whistles.*)

JENNY: (*Brisk.*) Come along, Mr Turner, that's quite enough jokes for today. You know what we've got to do, don't you?

TIM: (*Humbly.*) Yes, nurse.

JENNY: Well, then, hurry up. Don't keep me waiting.

TIM: Sorry, nurse.

JENNY: You don't want me to get cross with you, do you. You're not feeling very strong either, are you, Mr Turner?

TIM: No, nurse.

JENNY: Right, then. Let's watch ourselves and do exactly what we're told.

TIM: Yes, nurse. I will.

JENNY: Otherwise the consequences for you could be pretty nasty.

TIM: Promise, nurse.

JENNY: Into bed then. Sharp. Who's taken their rubber sheet off the bed?

TIM: I –

JENNY: You know what the rules are. Right! I'll remember that. What are you sniggering at?

TIM: Lord Knickers.

JENNY: What about him?

TIM: Family motto: Free to Bend. (*Lies on sofa.*)

JENNY: That's enough of your little jokes, Mr
Turner. I'm afraid I'm going to lose my temper
with you.

TIM: No! No!

(*JENNY grimly wheels over the surgical trolley, rolls on
gloves, and puts the screen round him. They both disappear
behind it.*)

JENNY: Now!

(*The sound of struggling, then a mounting, muffled yell.
A baby starts screaming.*)

(*Behind screen.*) Damn!

TIM: (*Behind screen.*) Is that ours?

JENNY: Of course it's ours. You stay there. (*She
goes to the bedroom and reappears, holding baby in
her arms.*)

TIM: Can I come out?

JENNY: No!

TIM: Please.

JENNY: No, I said!

TIM: I want a drink of water.

JENNY: You heard what I said. I don't want
any naughtiness. You'll do as you're told.
Like always.

(*Fade.*)

STANLEY: Who would have thought, least of all that
ordinary, happy young couple with their everyday
cares and worries, their two bonny babies, that
destiny was about to strike them such a cruel, and
horrifying blow?

As they sat in their little suburban home,
watching the telly, planning for the kiddies'
future, discussing the new light that needed
putting in the bathroom – all the homely concerns
of young people in love, how were they to know?

How could they have known. They were
innocent. And yet they were guilty. Guilty in
the eyes of men and God. Yet, who could not
wring pity from their heart at the hand Fate
had played them. (*Less rhetorical, more saloon-bar
style now.*) But this astonishing, human story
really began for me on the Friday night I went
into what we called the paper's branch office to
have a drink before going home. Ned, the news
editor, was there with his "school" all happily
gathered round him, like a lot of little chicks
round a hen. (*Settling down to be important.*)
There are always similar "schools" in Fleet
Street, and they usually form round some
executive by men who think that diamonds may
drop down one day from the copy on his desk.
I always liked Ned, and I respected him –
I considered him to be a magnificent journalist
and news editor. But I was never a member of
his "school". I think I'll have another one –
yes, double. I was probably a bit too successful
for Ned's liking. At that time I was very
successful indeed. Yes, and that didn't really
endear me. That's what the game's like. Fleet
Street loves a failure, and I certainly wasn't
a failure then. Why, if you take the trouble –
I suppose you'd think it a bore wouldn't you?
You're a bit bloody grand, aren't you? You
think I can't afford to pay for a round of
drinks, don't you! Well, you're bloody right,
I can't. But if you had the ordinary human
interest to look through the paper's files during
those six years you'd see I had twice the space,
twice the success, and twice the number of front
page stories, more than any other member of
the staff. What was I saying? Oh, yes. Little
Jenny Turner. Well, now. On the Friday night,
then, I gave my usual friendly nod to Ned and
everyone, and ordered a small beer. I was

standing at the bar, thinking. I think a lot when I'm drinking. I don't suppose you'd believe it, but I do. Well, presently the phone rings and Ned has his ear to it for about ten minutes. Suddenly, he beckons me over, and he says: "Off you go, Stan. Just your stuff. In Leicester, there's a happily married couple with two children. Name of Turner. Some clerk in the local Ministry of National Insurance has just tipped us off." (*Pause. He drinks, struggles to remember.*)

"It seems they're really brother and sister. Call at the cashier's and I'll give you a chit. If you get a move on you might get there before they find out themselves. Best thing, Stanley, would be if you could break the news to them yourself." So that's how I found myself in a suburban street in Leicester on a cold February night. The wind was howling away when I arrived.

Fade up on house. TIM is sitting in the living-room. He is wearing a black leather motorcycling outfit. Very sharp. Beside him is a cradle with a young baby in it. He is nursing another. In the room are all kinds of children's things: clothes drying on a horse, toys, rattles, etc.

TIM: Are you alright?
JENNY: (*Off.*) Just coming.
TIM: Gosh, I do like the weekend.
JENNY: (*Off.*) I know.
TIM: Don't be too long. I'm getting hot in this.
STANLEY: Tim seemed a nice, well-spoken boy. Quite well up in things for a boy of his background, I thought. He seemed to be something of an all-round athlete. Boxer – keen motorcyclist. Even took an interest in medicine, he told me. It was a pitiful sight, that little, untidy room with the kiddies' things all

over it. But they were happy. They looked proud
then, they could still lift their heads up high.
(*JENNY comes in wearing a very elaborate wedding dress.
She looks pregnant.*)

JENNY: Well?

TIM: (*Breathtaken.*) Marvellous. You look marvellous.

JENNY: What about the roses?

TIM: Super.

JENNY: Pink. Knicker pink. Plastic, I'm afraid.

TIM: Darling! (*Rises.*) It's marvellous.

JENNY: Wait till you see the rest.

TIM: I don't feel dressed properly.

JENNY: Never mind. We'll think of something.

TIM: Let's put the babies to bed. Shall we?

JENNY: Let's! (*Crosses to TIM, takes baby. TIM takes
cot and starts towards the bedroom.*) Quickly!

STANLEY: It fell to me to break in on their
simple happiness, and smash their dream world
to smithereens. I didn't relish it, I can tell you.
(*He rings the front doorbell.*)

TIM: Who the devil's that?

JENNY: Damn!

TIM: (*Calls out.*) Who is it?

STANLEY: My name is Williams. Stanley Williams.

TIM: What do you want?

STANLEY: Is that Mr Turner?

TIM: Yes.

STANLEY: I wonder if I could have a few words
with you and your wife?
(*TIM and JENNY look at each other, baffled.*)

TIM: I suppose we'll have to let him in. Here –
take the baby, will you?

JENNY: Just a minute. (*She lifts up her wedding
dress and pulls down her pregnant padding.*) OK.
(*She takes the baby. TIM opens the door.*)

STANLEY: Good evening. I'm sorry to bother you,
but – oh!
(*He stares at JENNY in her wedding dress and the baby.*)
Mrs Turner?

JENNY: Yes.

STANLEY: Oh, my God!

JENNY: What's the matter with him?

STANLEY: Forgive me. It was a shock. May I – may
I sit down for a moment?
(*JENNY kicks the padding out of sight. TIM shows him to
a chair.*)
Thank you, thank – well, I can tell you life has
dealt me some bad hands in my time but – I'm
sorry, but you don't have a drink, do you?
(*Fade.*)

*The dark figure of TIM is sitting sadly in the living-room. STANLEY,
JENNY, and the two CHILDREN leave through a window. As they
do so, the POSTMAN is at the front door, haggling with the
REPORTERS and CAMERAMEN over the price for the exclusive
right to the story. STANLEY, looking wary and paternal, ushers
JENNY and the CHILDREN downstage left, with him. He carries
a suitcase and one of the BABIES for her.*

STANLEY: I was glad to get out of that one I can
tell you. What sickened me was the way everyone
behaved. As if it were a cattle auction. I tell you,
I could have cheerfully seized hold of him and
broken his neck. Cringing, pleading, whining. It
was disgusting. (*To JENNY.*) You go round the
corner, my dear, and wait in my car. They won't
know you're gone.
(*She nods, takes the other BABY, and moves a few paces
downstage. STANLEY goes gravely over to the haggling group
at the door.*)

POSTMAN: Hello, I've been expecting you. Well,
now everybody's here, we can really get down to
business. I've got the girl, and I've got the babies.

1ST REPORTER: What about the husband?

POSTMAN: He doesn't matter. He's a bit mental,
if you ask me. I'll tell you now straight out. I'm
out to get the highest price I can. I'm strictly
a businessman.

STANLEY: Nonsense. You're a postman.

1ST REPORTER: Ha, ha, ha!

POSTMAN: The paper that bids the highest will get the story, that's all.

STANLEY: (*Righteously.*) What do you think this is? A cattle market?

POSTMAN: Alright – what's your bid, mate? (*STANLEY hesitates. Trying to look dignified. The other REPORTERS make three-figure offers.*)

1ST REPORTER: If you'll just wait half an hour until I can speak to my editor and get his OK, I'll double all these bids!

POSTMAN: (*To STANLEY.*) What's your bid?

2ND REPORTER: I'll pay more than him!

3RD REPORTER: How about two hundred quid, now, straight down in cash?

4TH REPORTER: Will you take a cheque?

3RD REPORTER: See, there it is. I've got it in my hand.

POSTMAN: Come on, you! I know you can afford it. Make your bid, then, or have you got to ask your boss first?

STANLEY: No, I don't. I'll make my bid now. Nothing! (*He summons himself up to a great moral occasion.*) And do you know why? Because I don't believe in all this trading in human beings. (*He begins to stalk away, and the haggling begins again. A REPORTER buttonholes him.*)

REPORTER: OK, Stanley. But just to cover me can I tell my office how much you paid for it? Can I say you've given £1,000? They won't go higher than five. Just to cover me.

STANLEY: You can tell your office I got it for free. (*REPORTER shrugs and moves off. STANLEY goes over to JENNY and takes the BABY.*) Listen, Jenny, I'm not going to promise you any money, but right now I'll take you and your babies out of this place, into a decent hotel

room where you can have a nice warm bath and
a meal. And then when you feel better we'll talk.
What do you say, Jenny?
(*JENNY looks blank.*)
She smiled through her tears and nodded.

JENNY: What about Tim?

STANLEY: He'll be alright. He won't leave that
house. To be honest with you, Jenny, he seems to
have a rather morbid obsession with the place,
especially your possessions. It's understandable,
I suppose – all the little things you'd bought
together. He did want to come with you at first,
but I talked him out of that. (*Away from her
again.*) Poor lad, he was so stunned, he couldn't
see right from wrong at first. Well, I phoned the
office and I said I can give you the exclusive
story of the girl who married her brother, signed
by her. I think you'll want to use it on page one.
(*Drop banner with headline* – I MARRIED MY
BROTHER.)
They did.

JENNY: I am the girl who married her brother.
Yes, the handsome man who is the father of my
two darling baby boys is my father's child, my
mother's son. Now that the tragic truth is out
I have decided to tell my full story – if only
because it might prevent such a terrible thing
happening again to anyone. It is the story of
years of happiness as man and wife. And it ends
with the most terrible day of my life – the day,
four months ago, when we realised that we were
the son and daughter of the same mother and
father. As all the world knows by now, my
brother, Timothy, and I were parted as children
by our mother's death. He went into a home, and
I was adopted by a Leicester couple.
I am still young. My life is before me. But I know
that my future must not, cannot, include the man
I love. Because the man I love is my brother.

STANLEY: I should have read her palm for her then. On the evening of the day that story was published, I introduced her to a young post office clerk. Two weeks later they were married. (*He leads JENNY and the children off.*)
(*Fade.*)

Fade up on wedding group with JENNY as the bride in white.

STANLEY: Well, Jenny asked to go to London, where she could lose her tragedy among the hundreds which London bears in her great heart every day. And sure enough she did – only too soon. I liked her choice. He seemed an admirably upstanding young man. Frankly, I certainly preferred him to Turner, who seemed a bit of an odd fish to me. There was something solid about this other boy, both feet on the ground. And, of course, nothing wrong or perverted – in the way the other relationship had been I mean.
(*During all this the happy group is being doused with rice, photographed, etc.*)
My first reaction was to talk them out of it.
I felt it might not be wise for two young people who had known each other such a short time to join themselves in Holy Matrimony. Especially as the young man was so respectable. I returned to the office and made my views known to the editor. He didn't agree with me. He said most impatiently, that if Jenny and this boy were in love and wanted to marry it was none of my business. What was my business, he was most explicit to point out, was to ensure that if they did marry, our paper should have the story of their wedding – with pictures – exclusively. It was a tough assignment. However, I was used to that. He gave me authority to pay the expenses of the wedding, to organise it, and to buy a trousseau for Jenny second to none. Oddly

enough this aspect of it seemed to fascinate her more than even the wedding itself. We spent days in lingerie shops. Anyway, the big day came round. Jenny was married with due solemnity – it was a specially moving occasion for all – and I was the best man. At the request of the groom, I thought that was rather nice of him.

(*A wedding reception is quickly improvised.*)

Jenny looked very lovely, I thought. Very beautiful and radiant indeed, with an enormous bouquet of pink roses. It's occasions like this that make my sort of job really worth doing. I arranged a slap-up reception, managed to dodge the other papers and everyone was happy. But I reckoned without my editor. The wedding of the girl who married her brother was too big to let pass like this. Well, I suppose people want to dig down so they can understand a little more.

(*Raises champagne glass.*)

To the happy couple.

BRIDEGROOM'S MOTHER: Oh, it is lovely, isn't it. We are grateful, you know. We'd never have been able to afford anything like this.

STANLEY: It's a pleasure, my dear. A pleasure to see such charming, delightful people blessed with such good fortune.

BRIDE'S MOTHER: (*To STANLEY.*) You will try and keep this out of the other papers, won't you, Mr Williams?

STANLEY: Don't you worry, it's all being taken care of.

(*A reporter and a photographer approach. STANLEY looks anxious.*)

Have some more champagne, my dear, with the paper's compliments. What are you two doing here?

REPORTER: Hello, Stanley. Seems we're on the same story.

STANLEY: What do you mean?

REPORTER: I've got Turner here.

STANLEY: Who?

REPORTER: The brother, Tim. The brother.

STANLEY: Sh! Where is he?

REPORTER: Outside in the car.

STANLEY: What's the angle?

REPORTER: The loneliest man in Britain watches
wedding on the outskirts of the crowd.

STANLEY: Listen, I don't know what you're up to, but
I've promised these people a serious nice wedding
– not a peep show. And I'm keeping to that.

REPORTER: Well, it's a good twist.

STANLEY: Damn your twist!

REPORTER: Relax, Stanley. You're drunk. You
only try to be moral when you're drunk.

STANLEY: These are nice people, and this is
a solemn and important day of their lives.
I won't have it made into a stunt.

REPORTER: Listen, Stanley, our instructions are
to get a picture of him congratulating the bride
and bridegroom.

STANLEY: But it's not possible. It just can't be
done. The young couple might allow it, perhaps
– though I'm not so sure. But what about Mum
and Dad?

REPORTER: That's your problem, Stanley.
Remember, we're waiting. (*Goes out.*)
(*STANLEY rejoins reception. He sweats. The
BRIDEGROOM'S FATHER concludes a speech.*)

FATHER: And in conclusion, I should like to
express our deep, heartfelt gratitude to the man
who made all this possible, a good and loyal
friend – Mr Stanley Williams.

STANLEY: (*Rises and raises glass.*) Ladies and
gentlemen. Now, I have a very special toast to
give. I want us to drink to a man who has
suffered a great sorrow, a good, kind man, who

must be feeling very lonely today. The older ones among us here, who watch the happiness of this wonderful young couple, do know that fate plays many strange tricks on men and women as they make their winding journey through life.

And the older folks here, I do know, would want me to make this toast, just to show, that in the hearts of none of us here lingers the slightest ill-feeling or hostility to the lonely man who, though he is not in our presence, must surely have been today in all our minds. Ladies and gentlemen, I give you a toast. To the brother of this lovely bride – to Timothy Turner.

BRIDEGROOM: To Timothy Turner.

(*All drink.*)

ALL: To Timothy Turner.

BRIDEGROOM: What a wonderful thought.

BRIDEGROOM'S MOTHER: To her brother. We certainly bear him no ill-will – to Timothy Turner.

ALL: To Timothy Turner.

(*A pause. STANLEY sweats and signals to a WAITER to refill the glasses.*)

STANLEY: It is indeed a great pity that the brother of the bride is not with us here today. I am certain that all of us here would have been willing to let him share a little of our happiness, if only he could have been present. I am confident that there is not one person in this room today who would not wish to shake his hand firmly, and wish him well.

BRIDEGROOM: I wish he were here. I'd like to shake him by the hand for one.

BRIDEGROOM'S MOTHER: So do I.

BRIDEGROOM'S FATHER: Yes.

BRIDEGROOM'S BROTHER: Hear, hear.

STANLEY: Well, ladies and gentlemen, he is here! At this moment he is wishing his sister and her bridegroom the very best of luck. He

hopes to be allowed to catch a glimpse of
the happy couple as we leave – (*Backs into
BRIDEGROOM'S BROTHER.*)

BRIDEGROOM'S BROTHER: Do you mind?

STANLEY: – just a glimpse from across the street.
(*STANLEY sits down. There is a terrible pause.*)

BRIDEGROOM'S MOTHER: Mr Williams, I think
you ought to go and fetch him.
(*STANLEY's eyes swim gratefully at her, then he goes off
right, coming back almost instantly with TIM.*)

JENNY: Tim!
(*He comes forward hesitantly, shakes hands with JENNY.
Flashbulbs flash. Cameras click. Everyone rushes forward to
greet TIM. He takes a glass of champagne, and toasts the
happy couple.*)

TIM: To the bride and groom.
(*Confusion. Cameras. Cries of "Hear, hear," "Well said,"
"Well done, old man." Someone starts to sing "For he's
a jolly good fellow." JENNY hands him a rose.*)

JENNY: You see the colour?

ALL: (*Sing.*) "For he's a jolly good fellow."
(*GUESTS go out. STANLEY crosses to TIM, puts a hand on
shoulder. TIM shrugs it off. STANLEY goes out. Car horns.
JENNY is swept off by her BRIDEGROOM and GUESTS,
her eyes glancing back at TIM.*)

STANLEY: Turner was warmly, fondly welcomed.
He shook hands with his sister, the mother of
his babies. He shook hands with the bridegroom.
Somebody gave him a glass of champagne and
he drank the happy couple's health. The best,
the newsiest, the most story-telling picture of
the year had been obtained for the paper. It was
splashed the following Sunday – the picture of
the uninvited guest at the wedding of the girl
who married her brother. And that was that.
(*The stage is clear by now except for the outline of the
TURNERS' house. It is dark.*)
Or that should have been that. That was nine
years ago. And now here I am outside that little

suburban house in Leicester, waiting for
a glimpse of the couple who have lived there,
these past seven years, never seeing anyone,
never even answering the door, leaving notes for
the tradesmen. I know who the man is; it's
Turner all right. But what about the woman with
him, locked up, day and night? Last week, this
newspaper went to find out. I can now state
quite definitely that the couple living there in
dark seclusion are Timothy Turner and his
sister, Jenny.
(*He bawls through the letter box.*)
Tim! Jenny! Tim! Jenny! Jenny! It's only old
Stanley. It's your pal, Stanley. Life hasn't been
too good to me either, you know. Give us
a break. Eh, Jenny. Come on. Be a pal. To old
Stan. (*Vexed.*) It's no good hiding, you know.
You've got to come out one day. You've got to
come out one day, and when you do, we'll be
waiting – Jenny!
(*Slips newspaper through door.*)
I put a copy of this issue through the door, just
to show them that the world is still interested in
them, and, yes, wants to help. To Timothy and
Jenny I leave this message. You can't escape the
world. Even if you want to, it won't let you.
Come out then, I say. Show yourselves. Be
brave. Be courageous. Fear not. Fear not.
(*STANLEY collapses, drunk and miserable. Dead possibly.*)

The End.

WATCH IT COME DOWN

Characters

SALLY PROSSER

BEN PROSSER

RAYMOND

GLEN

SHIRLEY

JO

MARION

DOCTOR ASHTON

Watch it Come Down was first performed by the National Theatre Company at the Old Vic, London on 24 February 1976, and then transferred to the Lyttleton Theatre on 20 March 1976 with the following cast:

SALLY PROSSER, Jill Bennett

BEN PROSSER, Frank Finlay

RAYMOND, Michael Feast

GLEN, Michael Gough

SHIRLEY, Angela Galbraith

JO, Susan Fleetwood

MARION, Rowena Cooper

DOCTOR ASHTON, Peter Needham

Director, Bill Bryden

ACT ONE

Scene 1

The action takes place in two separated areas of what was once a country railway station. At the back of the larger section is the door leading to the deserted platform and station, which can just be seen through one of the windows. Also deep countryside in distance. On one side, what was once the booking office has become a dining-room hatch. The main part of the set is obviously what was once the entrance to the station and waiting room. The smaller section, separated by a door, may have once been the parcels office. This is where GLEN is at present. Beside him, as he lies in a very large comfortable bed, covered in blankets and pillows, is a pile of books from which he is making notes. In fact, there are books everywhere, and in both main rooms, although more in GLEN's. Near him, in a comfortable old armchair is JO, reading and eating an apple. They both look content. She is strong-looking, about thirty-ish, sharp, open and with a spirit of natural inquiry about her. He is considerably older, with a comfortably frail look of some of those who lead a bookish life but there is an amiable fever there too.

In the main room, SALLY lies on a large rug talking to RAYMOND, who is propped nearby. She is somewhat older than JO, carelessly smart and definitive-looking in contrast to JO's glaring sloppiness which some might take to admiringly and others leave thankfully alone. RAYMOND is in his late thirties, the quiet, dog-of-all-work homosexual who pads reliably at the heels of others' lives.

The old station has been done up with some care but it doesn't quite come off. It's been made to be as comfortable as possible, almost like a penthouse in parts, but odd concessions have been made to its origins in the odd gas lamp here and there and the odd timetable or bench. There's even a touch of railway green in places. However, BEN has his say about this later. On one side, there is a set of steps, leading to BEN's mother's room. On the other one to SALLY and BEN's room. There are also doors to where SALLY's sister, SHIRLEY, works and sleeps. Also one for RAYMOND.

SALLY: Ben must have been barmy to buy this place.

RAYMOND: Well, it was cheap, right in the country, and lots of room for people.

SALLY: People! He hates "*people*". Who "lives" here? Me and him – if you call that living. His old mother so's he can shove her up above the booking office with her television and cats. His father because he didn't have to have *him* much either until he was dying and he started treating him like Tolstoy on *his* last platform. An academic old pouf who lies in bed most of the day writing waspish biographies to scandalise and titivate his friends who write for the weekly newspapers – when he's not being wise and famous and discreet with his boys in the old parcels office.

RAYMOND: He could still use the old "Gents" on the platform if he wanted.

SALLY: I expect he does. But he's the only one who's as nice and encouraging to Ben there is. Encouragement at his age and after what he's done! Most brilliant young director at Cannes, revolutionary. Even his Oscars didn't corrupt him! You're here, my sister's here because I can at least talk to *you,* when he can't or won't or doesn't. Jo's here because she looks after Glen and his "writing" and because she's the sort of randy tongue-in-the-lip romantic Ben thinks he missed out in his search for the Holy Groin. As long as he lusts after her he feels the odd flicker of life even if they do threaten the almighty constant standby power cut. You're here because he's doing me a favour having someone to talk to and he can feel generous and big too because he knows you don't go for girls. Also, he doesn't really like you. He only likes old-style, exotic or bitchy, brainy poufs. Shirley he allows to do her old painting here – which he more or less openly despises even to her – because he still has a daft, mystical itch that she might be the enigmatic tally to me. He doesn't really believe it, but it helps to flesh out a pretty dull scenario. If he did get to bed with her, he'd find acres of hand-picked, morning-fresh peas under that mattress! He doesn't want that kind of trouble even if he does toy about with it. It wouldn't be soft or cuddly for long. He's doing me a favour, letting me have girl-talk with my own sister through the two-way mirror, both so alike, both so different. The hard form of enigma! And me? Why am I here?

RAYMOND: You love him?

SALLY: Yes. Sort of. In a way. There's always been a tiny fuel in the tank. Or a dribble in the can to crawl home.

RAYMOND: Doesn't sound much fun.

SALLY: It isn't. Do you know what *is* fun any more? I used to think I did. It's rusted up. By people like Ben. All seriousness and newspapers. No frivolity. Not honest, easy, unthinking frivolity. How to be frivolous and impress everyone... I don't think I ever really liked him.

RAYMOND: You must have done.

SALLY: Why? People marry for love. You don't have to like 'em. That's Ben's mistake. I like you. Yes, and I love you. That's what's Ben's sure-fire one, this is it, wait for it: if your fag friends are so great and appreciative and affectionate and you can "talk" to them, why don't you –

RAYMOND: Marry them –

SALLY: Marry them! *Our* sex pitch has been washed out for years. Why don't you become a *real* married nun?

RAYMOND: I'm sorry.

SALLY: Oh, he exaggerates. So do I. "Rhetorical" he calls it. But *he does*. Some fishy self-importance about being Celtic or Coptic or something... Ending up in a self-conscious tarted-up Unlikely Homes Supplement railway station. What am I doing in a bloody railway station! A caravan

would be better. Intimate community living.
Nothing to do. Except bottle fruit and make vile
wine, like Jo, and try and explain ourselves to
odd journalists from comfortable houses in
Islington or Wembley why we're as barmy as
they think we are. "The Prossers, tired of the rat
race" – I wasn't tired, I was still in my stride –
"'decided to change their life style, get away
from it all as so many of us would like but lack
their initiative." Initiative! We could have had
a Palladian gem for the graft we bled out to
bolshy, careless, barricade-minded builders for
this railway folk-weavers' folly. No-one to see...
I almost wish Will Hay would walk in with
Graham Moffat under his arm. Except that Ben
would go into some mad, menopausal ecstasy and
then I'd *have* to leave. I wish the trains *did* still
come through. I could throw ham rolls at
the passengers.

RAYMOND: There's still one a week.

SALLY: Only a goods train and that's closing
down next month. Ben says then he can get on
landscaping the gardens. Gnomesville Halt!
Water gardens from the ladies' loo and potted
plants in the signal box.

(*A small train goes through.*)

RAYMOND: Well, *there's* your weekly ghost train.

SALLY: Get *out,* someone! Even if you're a ghost!
Ben'll be home soon.

RAYMOND: Would you like me to tell the
others first?

SALLY: What? About us separating? Ben and me?

RAYMOND: Yes.

SALLY: Sure.

RAYMOND: You've made up your mind?

SALLY: Yes. Tell my sister. Tell Jo; she'll love it,
tell Glen. Needn't bother with Ben's ma. It won't
worry her, just so long as her cats are fed and
the telly's working.

RAYMOND: I just wondered.

SALLY: What?

RAYMOND: Well, as it isn't *true*. About you
both separating.

SALLY: Who knows? It might be. It almost is. Perhaps
it will be. Perhaps they'll all jolly it along. Should
be interesting. Their concern, I mean.

RAYMOND: Has Ben agreed?

SALLY: Not really. Of course, he's intrigued with
the situation but he has heavy moral scruples,
oh, all about putting one's friends to the test and
conspiring against them and playing some
hideous truth game...

RAYMOND: Then perhaps I shouldn't.

SALLY: You do what *I* say. And act as *if you* think
it's true.

RAYMOND: *Should* I!

SALLY: Why not? He doesn't like you? You'd better
tell my sister first. I can get her out of the way
more easily. Then Jo and Glen. And make sure
they're all going to be very English and discreet.
Not that they won't be all looking like a bunch of
misused basset hounds. Can't wait for his ex-wife
to find out. Marion'll be down like a *shot* if she
can. I wonder if she went to lunch with him and
the child today. Not that he'll tell me the truth.
Where is he? Probably mooning over the old
boy's grave after a touching lunch with his
small daughter.
(*Enter BEN from the platform. He is in his mid-forties with
the look of a man who has tried fitfully to look younger but
only partially succeeded.*)
Lunch alright then?

BEN: Alright then. Whatever that means.
Hello, Raymond.

SALLY: What about me?

BEN: What about you?

SALLY: Yes. Well, a kiss or just "Hello darling,
couldn't wait to get back..."

BEN: Oh, I could wait alright. I spend my
life waiting.

SALLY: So you say...

BEN: Like Queen Victoria you always lead from
well in front.

SALLY: Oh, blooming quotations. One of Glen's,
I suppose.

BEN: Yes, another. Better than your unlistening,
constant rant.

SALLY: My –

BEN: To continue –

SALLY: Oh, we have had a bad day...

BEN: Like Melbourne, you have great capacity for
love. And nowhere to put it.

SALLY: Thanks a hump. (*To RAYMOND.*) Impressed?
He's read a book.

BEN: And forgotten them all.

SALLY: Well, they certainly didn't teach you
anything. A spot of gardening would have done
you more good...

BEN: You only accept love. You can't respond to it...

SALLY: Do shut that bloody door. That platform's like
a wind tunnel. You always come back pompous
when you've been to London. Why didn't you buy
a new set of gear, a suit or a new shirt?

BEN: I didn't have time.

SALLY: Well, you are getting too portly for
clothes, I'll agree. You're boring poor little
Raymond and he's been such fun.

BEN: Gay, you mean.

SALLY: Oh, shut up, bitch-face.

BEN: We know what that's like. Being GAY.
Whoops! The shroud of spontaneity!

SALLY: Don't overdo it. At your age, you can't.
Anyway, it makes *you* look like a *real* pouf.

BEN: I'm sure. It could fool *you*! Sorry, Raymond.

SALLY: You're not sorry. You like saying hurtful
things. They require no effort. You're just boring
him. And what's worse, me. The minute you get in.

BEN: Sorry. Carry on carousing.

SALLY: You've put the clappers on that alright.

BEN: I've had a long day.

SALLY: All the days are long the way we live. It must be something to do with the shifting ice-cap. Or maybe it's just you?

BEN: Oh, knock it off for five minutes. Do your cabaret somewhere else.

SALLY: You wouldn't believe it but it goes down quite well with some people.

BEN: Oh, I believe. There's always a public for vulgarity and cruelty if it's put over well. Try the working men's clubs. Or the Black Rhinoceros; a literary lunch; or an evening at *Giselle*.

SALLY: Giselle – 'e's 'ell.

BEN: *I* thought that was funny when *you* were learning to make omelettes and speak French in Switzerland on Daddy's hard-inherited shareholdings.

SALLY: Don't leer at my father. At least he was brave and never whined.

BEN: Perhaps he should have. Anyway, I liked him. Oh, here we go...

SALLY: Yes, here we go. Mr Wonderful Wise Man. Anyway, he didn't like you.

BEN: So you say. Often. It doesn't really matter.

SALLY: No, he's dead. He saw through you.

BEN: Well, he was successful on the stock market and the racecourse.

SALLY: Why shouldn't he be? He was bright and interested in things.

BEN: He was. Is there a drink?

SALLY: At least *he* could hold his liquor. The *hard* stuff. Not like you.

BEN: I remember. The Colonial Service was the spearhead of his chota pegs.

SALLY: Oh, not that! At least we didn't all slobber ourselves to death with requiems and odious

music hall songs at *his* funeral. I suppose you
had a misty-eyed butchers at his grave on the
way back?

BEN: I looked in. Dammit, it's only a month.

RAYMOND: Here's a drink.

BEN: Thanks.

SALLY: "And yet within a month." Well, say "thank
you" properly.

BEN: I don't know what "properly" is.

SALLY: Evidently. But don't brag about it. My
father was *interested*.

BEN: He was.

SALLY: I don't know why. He wouldn't be now.

BEN: Just as well he's not here then. Cheers to
the departed!

SALLY: Getting all those people down to that
sickening funeral. He *died*; that's all. Not before
time. I think even *he'd* have been embarrassed at
your turning it into a Ben Prosser production.

BEN: He liked a bit of carnival, anyway.

SALLY: Boozing and sponging you mean. He didn't
even like *you*.

BEN: No?

SALLY: No.

BEN: What do *you* know about it?

SALLY: A lot. He used to talk to me quite often. In
an incoherent, illiterate sort of way.

BEN: Did he? Is this for Raymond's entertainment
or mine?

RAYMOND: I'll pop upstairs.

SALLY: No, you stay. Just because His Regisseur
Droopy Drawers has dropped in.

RAYMOND: I've got to see Shirley.

BEN: No, no, stay. You can see what she has to put
up with...

SALLY: We've *all* had a long day. Get *me* a drink,
Raymond, darling.

BEN: Darling!

SALLY: What's wrong with that – darling? (*Pause.*)
Let me take your coat off.
(*He looks at her suspiciously but lets her do so.*)
Mustn't let you get yourself cold...
(*RAYMOND gives SALLY a drink.*)
RAYMOND: How was the journey then?
BEN: Oh, fine. Had a row with that Major Bluenose.
RAYMOND: What about?
BEN: Oh, usual. If he and his wife see any of our
dogs on their land, etc., he's offered £5 to any
of his men who shoots one.
RAYMOND: Lovable man.
BEN: Oh and our cats worry his sheep. Sheep! And
his heifers! And some stuff about layabouts
lolling about here.
RAYMOND: Layabouts! What about those yobbos
smashing up the windows here last month? Bet
he arranged that.
BEN: Living in the country! All ex-housemasters,
rear admirals, prying vicars, prowling group
captains, ladies with walking sticks and scarves,
tombolas, pony events and the *Daily Telegraph.*
And they wonder why we won't go to their
sherry parties! Sherry!
SALLY: I don't know why you're surprised. I grew
up in it. The people are just more common and
self-conscious, that's all. After all, it *was* your
idea to get away from the messianic miseries of
metropolitan Albion. The town is *people* and
having to *give way.* The country's not green much
and rarely pleasant. Land is bad for people. The
green belt of muddied, grasping, well-off peasants
from public schools and merchant banks.
BEN: Look who's talking!
SALLY: *I* know what I'm talking about. With
shotguns in the woods, tea and pearls, rural
swank and a tub of money under the chintz
four-poster. Fêtes opened by local TV celebrities,

restoration funds, old ducks who "come in
and do", village greens, hunting "manners",
indifferent food and pewter candlesticks,
over-healthy children home for the hols, greedy
Gorgon nannies, undergraduates fumbling
behind bushes of floodlit lawns, dancing till
dawn with Miss Sarah Crumpet-Nicely of
Grasping Hall while Mummy and Daddy look on
at all the young people "having such a good
time" against this nasty, brutish issue of English
Country Life. No, there's not much life in the
land. Fish and animals yes; and the pigs who
own it and *run* it.

RAYMOND: Well, can't say I've seen much of that.

SALLY: Don't worry. You won't. Except as somebody's
bit of a lark. Not a lower-middle-class pouf
from Leicester and living with a lot of nuts
in a railway station. No, land is for the truly
covetous. They'll even let armies of Japs and
Texans loose on it to slaughter the pheasant, the
grouse and the deer and have a wildlife Vietnam
of their own to keep what they've got. Mindless
millionaires wading in the jungle warfare of the
new-style trout stream –

BEN: I think you've made your point. I'm almost
beginning to see theirs.

SALLY: You would. You're a snob.

BEN: Yes. Could I have another, Raymond?

SALLY: Why can't you get it yourself? What is he
– the butler?

BEN: Only for some, I dare say. (*He goes to refill
his glass.*)
(*Pause.*)

SALLY: And how was lunch with your little daughter?

BEN: She's not little – as you know. She's 11 years
old and over five feet tall.

SALLY: Really. I forgot. I'm surprised *you*
remembered. Well?

BEN: Well, what?

SALLY: Lunch. *The* lunch with little – sorry, *tall* – *fruit* of your tired old loins?

BEN: Look! I'm just back. Do we have to keep this up straight away?

SALLY: Sorry. Did you say *get* it up or *keep* it up?

BEN: Getting coarse a bit early, aren't we?

SALLY: As usual, I take my cue from you.

BEN: Cue. The only cue I'd give you is a billiard cue. To break over your head. I'm tired.

SALLY: So am I. You *must* think of others.

BEN: I have.

SALLY: And I thought your memory had almost failed altogether. What did she eat? Five feet one. Face like a bun.

BEN: I don't know. It can't interest you.

SALLY: Of course it does. I wouldn't want to have a round little – sorry, *tall* round – step-daughter.

BEN: Steak, spaghetti, ice-cream and coke. Alright?

SALLY: Bad for the figure and the teeth I'd say.

BEN: It's what she wanted. It wasn't for me to argue.

SALLY: You're her *daddy*, aren't you? But it's hard for you to come down even a bit heavy. After all, you did leave her – a little – a little tall – baby for a lady who wasn't her mummy. *And* who's only a step-mummy.

BEN: You're hurting yourself...

SALLY: No, I'm not. I'm past all that long ago.

BEN: Well, perhaps I'm not.

SALLY: Ah... Did you see her *Mummy*? Mummy: very attractive, in a stunted sort of way.

BEN: Stop it, Sally!

SALLY: Stop what?

RAYMOND: Another drink?

SALLY: Yes. Give the Master another drink. He's had a hard day. Mummy's a very witty woman at the dinner table. She says things like "Hemingway's mind was never raped by an idea." Awfully good. She says it quite often too... Did you fuck her?

BEN: No...

SALLY: Pity. It might have cheered you up. Before
coming back to Country Life Halt and old Dad's
grave. I'm sorry you didn't enjoy your lunch
à deux. Not much to say to one another?

BEN: Damn it, I only see her about three times
a year...

SALLY: Difficult to communicate? That's sad. There
are so many things little girls are interested in.
Especially when their daddies are famous, like
film directors. I always find she never stops
chattering when she's with me.

BEN: I've no doubt.

SALLY: Perhaps you've never cared for the secret
of getting through to other people – even little
girls. Even your own tall little girl... Or perhaps
she doesn't *like* you. Just that... A lot of people
don't, you know...

BEN: Will you, you, will you, for one minute, just
stop that fucking pile of shit spewing out of
your fucking mouth!

SALLY: A hit, Raymond. I say: a *palpable*!

BEN: Or you'll get my fist right in the fucking
middle of it. From my puny fist even if it breaks
my arm...

SALLY: You mustn't damage your arm... Can *I* have
another drink?

BEN: I'm sorry.

SALLY: No, I'm *sorry*. I shouldn't have said those
things. It's my fault.

BEN: I – I, well, bad time... But I bought you
a present...

SALLY: Thank you. That was sweet of you. I'll
open it after I've, I've had this...
(*She takes a drink from RAYMOND. BEN gets his package.
SALLY sips the drink and slowly slides into a low moan of
tears. BEN looks on. RAYMOND puts his arm round her –
nods to BEN, who slowly puts down the package, and walks*

upstairs to their room. He hesitates half-way, as if to go back over to her. As he starts back, SHIRLEY appears from her doorway, closely followed by JO. When BEN sees them he returns back up to the room. RAYMOND looks round quickly and motions both girls back. SHIRLEY also falters but then goes back. JO, however, stands watching the scene for a few moments without moving. Then slowly, she goes back into her room, closing the door behind her. GLEN looks up.)

GLEN: Anything the matter?

JO: Nothing... I'll get us some tea in a minute. (*She strokes his hand.*) Glen, darling...

GLEN: What's that?

JO: You really are so very gentle...
   (*He pats her hand affectionately. Meanwhile, RAYMOND comforts the collapsed SALLY.*)
   (*Curtain.*)

Scene 2

Shortly after.

RAYMOND comes down the stairs from SHIRLEY's room. JO, unseen, is in the kitchen preparing GLEN's tea. SHIRLEY is upstairs in her room. So is BEN's MUM: vague telly sounds. Her voice calls out, "Ben, Ben! Are you back? Where is everyone... Is there a cup of tea? Cup of tea?..." Then silence. RAYMOND looks around, then looks to GLEN's door. He knocks.

RAYMOND: Am I interrupting?

GLEN: (*Rising and picking out a couple of books from the surrounding piles.*) No, come in.

RAYMOND: Thought you'd be kipping.

GLEN: Not a bit. As a matter of fact, I think I'm on the last page of my book.

RAYMOND: Then I'd better leave it.

GLEN: No, don't, my dear. After 1,200 pages and three years I should know where I'm at. The most enjoyable bit. Topping it off with the right coda, *and* knowing what it is... Something's wrong, isn't it?

RAYMOND: Yes.

GLEN: Sally and Ben?

(*He returns to his sofa and box with books and manuscript.*)

RAYMOND: Yes.

GLEN: We heard them scrapping of course. But it didn't sound special. Well, of course it's always *special*. We're all that... What is it?

RAYMOND: They're splitting up.

GLEN: Again?

RAYMOND: Yes, but *really*.

GLEN: What will they do?

RAYMOND: She's leaving... You know how she hates this place.

GLEN: I've heard her say so. But I thought she liked this bizarre warren enough to stick it out. I always thought the country was good for novelists... Not women perhaps.

RAYMOND: She says she hates the land.

GLEN: Ah, I know what she means. It doesn't always bring out the best in us. Suspicion, cupidity, complacency, hostility, profiteering, small, greedy passions, tweedy romance, all that. Beef barons, pig and veal concentration camps, Bentleys and pony traps and wellies. The Country. It's the last of England for *them,* the one last, surviving colony. This is England, all the merchants and adventurers and district officers have all come back. They don't want a new flag going up, a new name for their nation, all coal fields and oil riggers, Coventry, plastic factories and Dagenham Man. The fuzzy wuzzies from Durham and the Rhondda are at the last gate... How *did* it happen? They needed one another. But no more. Who's going?... Is this really *it* this time?

RAYMOND: Sally? Seems certain.

GLEN: Certainly it's no place for an intellectual like Sally. Or Ben. Where do any of us go now? When I started this book I thought we all still needed what was even left.

RAYMOND: You and Jo love it here.

GLEN: I had my salon life in London which could accommodate everything, the metropolis *and* the country as well as blimps and lefties – the snobberies of both. Enough good food, drink, sex, drama, gossip, frivolity, gravity, friendship, bitching and charity which dared to speak its name. *Ah, Albion qui n'ose pas parler son nom.*

RAYMOND: You know I don't speak French.

GLEN: Just as well. A harsh way of saying commonplace things. Of making platitudes sound like paradoxes. I've been guilty of doing it all my life. It was only a precious bon-bon which I'd never dare even utter to Ben... So, it *does* all fall apart. Hardly surprising when there's hardly ever been a centre and certainly not ours. We've seen the future *and it doesn't work...* I might give *that* to Ben. He'd like the sentiment anyway. I think I shall take a rest somewhere. Where can one afford to? Even a bachelor, like me, with no responsibilities. Die? That's pretty expensive if you're not snappy about it. I haven't the energy for suicide. I don't mind the melodrama because mercifully one doesn't have to witness it.

RAYMOND: Don't joke, please, Glen.

GLEN: Armageddon's a better laugh than Dunkirk. Do they *really* –

RAYMOND: Yes. What about Jo?

GLEN: She doesn't need to care for me. Oh, she needs to love me. But she needs real love. While there's time left for it. Not just sex. She's open to anything. It's her magic and her misfortune. But magic more, far, far more. Sally can write a novel about her life with Ben in between cocktail parties and love affairs. Ben can brood over whether to ever direct another film for the next mere anarchy. And whether to send that vile old mother off to a senior citizens' home at last and

kill off her vile pussycats, have an affair with
Jo or Shirley or Jo and Shirley, go back to his
ex-wife – which I hope he doesn't – or just
blunder into some other form of chaos. *You* can
go back to the rag trade, I suppose. Or will you
stay with Sally?

RAYMOND: What do you mean?

GLEN: Stay with Sally?

RAYMOND: I don't know what you mean. I came
here to look after Sally and Ben, do the cooking,
shopping, household chores, the animals. What
are you getting at?

GLEN: I can't see you doing the same thing with
Ben on his own. With *both,* yes. So, will you stay
with Sally?

RAYMOND: She hasn't asked me.

GLEN: I'm sure she will. There'll be other Bens. If
she does go.

RAYMOND: Well, I just, well, I was asked to tell you.

GLEN: By Sally?

RAYMOND: Yes.

GLEN: Does Ben know?

RAYMOND: I think so. I haven't spoken to him.

GLEN: I see. Am I to refer to it? Or carry on
as usual?

RAYMOND: I don't know.

GLEN: Ah: play it by ear. A bad option for me.
I can't abide conspiracies.

RAYMOND: Well, I'll let you finish.

GLEN: It's only another book. Books are an
outmoded form of communication. Probably
fascist from what I hear from my old University.
Perhaps they could turn it into an old folks'
home for people like Ben's Mum. Think how
they'd enjoy sitting in their wheelchairs in the
College Gardens and watching telly in the
Senior Common Room.

RAYMOND: Trouble is you're a snob. Even if you
do like taking home guardsmen.

GLEN: Of course I'm a snob. Just like some people are pigeon-fanciers. And young guardsmen, believe me, Raymond, have always been the fancy of many an upper class queen. It does take a certain amount of coinage – like marriage. At least, guardsmen are smart, alert, with bodies like fleshed-out greyhounds. That's how I got my beautiful family nose broken and the stitches over my eye. That's why I never fancied you, Raymond. Just tight trousers, a bad, working-class skin, all huff and pouf.

RAYMOND: *Some* people like it.

GLEN: Some people will put it in a brick wall, I believe.

RAYMOND: Finish your bloody old book. I've done my job.

GLEN: Who else have you told?

RAYMOND: Shirley.

GLEN: Ah, yes. *Painting* at her painting. Isn't it time she had another rally? Or stuck humanity's sharp banner up some police horses' inciting arseholes?

RAYMOND: Yes, you *are* a pig. I like her paintings; they're violent. They're about *now*!

GLEN: It must be a paler point in history than I thought. And my coda *is* wrong.

RAYMOND: You're an old, old-before-your-time pouf pig, stewing about in past glories and handing down all that in lofty 100-page indexes.

GLEN: You've been peeking. Found your tongue today. Not Sally's.

RAYMOND: *I* know what I think.

GLEN: What about Jo?

RAYMOND: She's my next.

GLEN: Just a moment –

RAYMOND: What?

GLEN: No. We must all know. I'm sorry I was rude, Raymond. You see, although I quite like

143

you, in spite of what I said – that was the everyday bitching you understand. Men and women are often very unsafe indeed together. Being page to a Lady and her Knight is a strange occupation... And, and I just don't trust you.

RAYMOND: You think I trust you? You're too bloody good and clever to live. Making everyone feel so *good* when they're with you. I don't know what they see in you. You're just a fork-tongued, lizardly, posh old pouf to me.

GLEN: It's true perhaps; what I know I lacked in humour I tried to make up for in wit.

RAYMOND: Thanks for the apology.

GLEN: You were only doing your job. Bearing your errand. Perhaps it's because I find you so ineffably unattractive. It's a fault *we* all share, I'm afraid.

(*RAYMOND goes out and GLEN returns to his manuscript. SALLY and BEN appear from their room. She is carrying BEN's package.*)

SALLY: Did you tell him?

RAYMOND: Yes.

SALLY: How'd he take it? Was he sorry?

RAYMOND: I don't know what goes on in his mind. Perhaps he was just thinking of his old book. He was just bitchy to me.

SALLY: Doesn't surprise me. Doesn't know how he's supposed to react with the least intrusion on his comfy academic hibernation. Shirley?

RAYMOND: Very upset. Burst into floods. Stopped painting. Said she'd talk to both of you whenever you'd like her to.

BEN: Christ! Revelations!

SALLY: That's something. Jo?

RAYMOND: Just going now. She's in the kitchen getting the Professor's whole wheatgerm natural honey and tea.

SALLY: Good. *She'll* be pleased. Hurry up.
  (*He goes.*)
  Now I'm going to see what you took the
  trouble to –
BEN: Don't you think you should try it on in
  the bedroom?
SALLY: Why? I *know* what it is. I saw it in *Vogue*.
  I'll just put the top on. Anyway, why shouldn't
  you buy me a present?
BEN: Well –
SALLY: Well, what?
BEN: It might seem a bit inappropriate. I mean, if
  we're supposed to be separating.
SALLY: I don't see why. I should still expect you to
  send me presents. And, if we should go ahead
  with it, I'll probably send you something quite
  expensive, like a Sulka dressing gown or a shirt
  from Turnbull and Asser. What will you send me?
BEN: A bar of carbolic, I should think. Good for
  the inside of the mouth.
SALLY: You were always unforgiving.
BEN: You need real stamina for the forgiving
  you've got in mind.
SALLY: Well, you certainly don't have it.
BEN: No, I don't. Oh, try it on.
SALLY: Darling, it's ravishing. Perfect. They're
  just *in* now.
BEN: Is that good?
SALLY: Oh, you always want the day before
  yesterday's fashion. Isn't it divine? Do you
  think this is the right colour for me?
BEN: Yes, that's why I chose it.
SALLY: Oh, don't be like that. Do you?
BEN: Well, I can get the other one.
SALLY: No. If you're not interested – no, I've
  decided this is the one. Darling, thank you, how
  clever you are... What good taste you have.
BEN: Oh, I thought you said my taste in all things
  was execrable.

SALLY: You're making it up. In women perhaps.
Anyway I wouldn't use a pompous word like
execrable. *You* sound pretty funny saying it.
More like Glen.
(*JO comes in with tea tray.*)

JO: Oh, sorry.

SALLY: Jo – darling – come in. Look what Ben
brought me back! Wasn't it clever of him? Just
what I wanted.

JO: It's beautiful. You always seem to know where
to go for Sally's clothes.

BEN: We have costumiers and wardrobe mistresses
in movies, you know. The last movie I made just
about paid off the wardrobe. That's all, in fact.

JO: Still – it's spiffing.

SALLY: Colour right, do you think?

JO: Bang on.

SALLY: Ben wasn't sure. This cut's just right for
my shoulders. You have to have the shoulders.
Hopeless if you're all round. Just make you look
gi-normous. Feel it. The stitching.

JO: I certainly will. I'll just take Glen in his tea. He's
had no lunch again. Too much work I suppose.

SALLY: I'll wear the whole thing tonight for dinner.
All wrong here – but you could just about go
anywhere in it, couldn't you? I'm so *tired* of all my
clothes down here. Same old thing, all the time.

JO: See you in a minute.
(*She goes into GLEN's room. Inside she puts down the tray.
She feels his forehead, kisses it. Then sits down to watch
him sleep.*)

SALLY: Looks as if *she* could do with something new.
But I expect you like all that woolly skirt and
shawl bit. Perhaps they'll bring back the dirndl
just for you. (*She puts the skirt up to her and watches
in the mirror.*) Fabulous. Ben, you're a miracle.
(*She kisses him. SHIRLEY appears at her door at this moment.*)

BEN: Just glad you like it.

SALLY: I'm sorry I said all that. Unforgivable.
Don't tell me how much it was.
(*SHIRLEY disappears, unseen to them.*)

BEN: They *were* pretty unforgivable.

SALLY: I *have* apologised.

BEN: As the truck said to the corpse. They
were unforgivable.

SALLY: What else can I do? Why did you give me
the bloody outfit then? To make me feel bad? Or
just plain old guilt?

BEN: Neither. I've given up guilt many a long Lent
ago. And I don't think I'd be able to make *you*
feel bad.

SALLY: Just yourself bad? *More* bad.

BEN: They're all past habits.

SALLY: Better than some of your other habits.

BEN: Anyway. I'm glad you liked it.

SALLY: Are you really? Glad?

BEN: If it gives you pleasure.

SALLY: God, you sound pious! You look like some
foul-minded stained old monk.

BEN: It might look a bit odd –

SALLY: Odd? You mean I don't look good enough
in it?

BEN: You look splendid.

SALLY: You're afraid of what your precious friends
will think?

BEN: I mean it's just a bit odd when they've just
been told we're splitting up at last.

SALLY: You mean we *are* splitting up?

BEN: *They* think we are.

SALLY: *They* think you're odd enough already.

BEN: But not *you*.

SALLY: At least *I'm* alive.

BEN: Bully for you!

SALLY: You're just a hulk. Alright, I *won't* wear it.
I'll wear a kaftan and prayer beads and look like
one of those virginal young nymphomaniacs.
It's pathetic!

BEN: Hear bloody hear! Listening to you is.

SALLY: All you scared, failing, middle-aged men. Memory-laneing for young brides, all of you. Nauseating. Why don't you grow up?

BEN: Why don't *you?* Men may become little boys but women never become little girls. It's why they lack the charm of a past life.

SALLY: Oh, good! Sound very appealing to the slavering males from the nose-job and mouth twenty-year-old, twenty-year-old plastic tit and bum dolly in your next carnival of melancholy movie. I can just see it. It's your wallets they're after, diddums, not your paunch, flabby old winkle and profile in depth, sight and sound.

BEN: You're the one who can't face the future.

SALLY: At least I don't mewl over the past, playing pat-a-cake with my past, saying I'm an *artist.*

BEN: I've never called myself an artist and you know it.

SALLY: Well, you *act* the part – very badly, I may say. Heavy performance. (*Yawns.*)

BEN: I've told you, I'm not even second rate. I'm third rate and pretty suspect at that.

SALLY: You're *second* rate. Like degrees at Oxford. Not clever enough to be careless First or imaginative and high-spirited enough to scrape yourself a Third.

BEN: What is today? Curse again? You're the only woman I know who has it 28 days a month.

SALLY: Barren, you mean?

BEN: Barren in spirit.

SALLY: The only spirit you'd know comes in two bottles daily.

BEN: Preferable to *your* high spirits. What's so special today then, Miss Jackboots?

SALLY: You can't hurt *me.*

BEN: I couldn't. That was the first thing I gave up. Or is it the oncoming hot flushes?

148

SALLY: Take a look at your own face. Flushed with booze and your self, your oozing, soggy self. Believe me –

BEN: If men had to go through –

SALLY: It's the men-o-pause. Alright. Male menopause. God, you must have had it along with your acne when you were lighter. A pretty sight. Hasn't even cleared up now. Pockmarks and veins. *You* gave in years ago. I'm just beginning! Whee!

BEN: Good. Clearly suits you.

SALLY: Were you going to say something? What was it? My complexion, my hair, my tits? Let me tell you I wear the same bra I wore 20 years ago.

BEN: What were you – in the Brigade of Guards?

SALLY: You mean I'm flat-chested?

BEN: Flat-headed.

SALLY: I'm not one of your cuddly little armfuls.

BEN: No, you're not. But some people like to embrace pythons round their necks.

SALLY: See what they're like when they're 30: boobs, round thighs and arses you could stick a telephone directory...

BEN: Sense of humour? If not proportion?

SALLY: You're the one with no sense of humour. Except for your same old jokes. The only joke you don't see is yourself.

BEN: You should have been a writer.

SALLY: You should have been a film director.

BEN: Ta.

SALLY: I *am* a writer.

BEN: Of Broadway comedies?

SALLY: You know – novels.

BEN: Short stories. Listen –

SALLY: (*Mimics.*) "Listen."

BEN: I've thrown better writers than you off TV commercials. *Men* writers. You need more than a resentful memory to be a writer.

SALLY: Oh, what do you know about it.

BEN: Then don't wear the bloody thing!

(*He snatches the new outfit from her and flings it right across the room. She looks at him calmly and then goes and picks them up, folding them and carefully packing them back in the box.*)

SALLY: If you're trying to attempt impressive gestures, remember that largeness demands needle control. That's why they upset you when they say your pictures are formless, self-indulgent and undisciplined.

(*Presently, he goes to her.*)

Anyway, it's a size too large.

BEN: No. I checked.

SALLY: You *checked*! Oh, yes, right for once...

BEN: Do wear it this evening.

SALLY: I'm going out this evening.

BEN: Who with?

SALLY: I don't know yet. No-one round here. Shirley. No, she'll be all heavy-lidded about our tragic separation. That and some new set of refugees.

BEN: Oh, Raymond. Of course...

SALLY: I might. There *is* that nice young farmer who rides so beautifully. *He* keeps ringing.

BEN: *Does* he?

SALLY: *He* didn't come from the back streets of Swansea to settle in Hammersmith. He *knows* a bit of class.

BEN: Ah, we revert! So, the Country Lifers really are Britain's spinal cord, after all.

SALLY: Some spine with a little wine would be fine. Can't face another homespun dinner with you lot.

BEN: Leaving me to it, eh?

SALLY: You'll cope. Think how sorry they'll be for you. Left all alone...

BEN: Sally, *I'm* sorry –

SALLY: No, you're not. You just *lost*.

(*He goes to touch her.*)

You've begun to smell...

(*RAYMOND enters with tea tray.*)

Physically. I can smell you in bed. And now in here...

Mum's tea?

(*RAYMOND nods.*)

Let him take it up to her himself.

RAYMOND: No. It's alright. I've got it now.

(*He proceeds upstairs.*)

SALLY: He's afraid to go himself. And lazy. Can't stand the sight of her. Not surprised. Tell her to put her teeth in if she ever comes down. Not that she will. Still, you can understand – like, where he gets *his* narrow, squinty eyes from. Oh, no, the old man had those too. Very Welsh that. At least he's not proud of *that*. Dinner out somewhere, dolly, Raymond. We could have a bit of a dance or something.

RAYMOND: Sure. But what about –

SALLY: The Refectory Party can amuse themselves tonight. We might even dress up and go to London. Would you hate it, Ben? Your wife with a pouf? After all, I'm leaving you with *yours*. Only he's more distinguished than mine.

BEN: Suit yourself. You *will*...

(*RAYMOND disappears. Pause.*)

I brought you your weeklies and magazines, and books you asked for.

SALLY: Thanks.

BEN: Thanks for the thanks.

(*RAYMOND reappears.*)

SALLY: How is the old crone?

RAYMOND: OK. Feeding the cats. She's having a tray in her room as usual.

SALLY: (*To BEN.*) Job for you – son.

BEN: (*Sings.*)

"At seventeen he fell in love quite madly
With eyes of a tender blue,
At twenty-four..."

151

SALLY: "He groaned along once more."
Can't you shut up?
BEN: No. Can you?
"At thirty-five he..."
SALLY: "He's still alive..."
BEN: Di di da – di da, etc.
"But it's when he thinks he's past love – "
SALLY: He *is*.
(*They sing together.*)
SALLY/BEN: "And he loves her as *he's never
loved before*."
SALLY: And bully for him! Couldn't have been much
cop at 17. As for *past* love. Poor girl!
BEN: I don't know. Might have a civilising influence
on her.
RAYMOND: I'll go and start some of the
dinner. Vegetables...
SALLY: Why should you? Let Jo do it. She's the
young lady who lives in a shoe.
(*RAYMOND goes out quickly.*)
BEN: They do say –
SALLY: They? Who's they?
BEN: They – the people *you* like to read in those
magazines, showing off about the novels they've
read, films, plays, and poetry. They, they say
some people live their art while others merely
create it. When are you going to write yours out?
SALLY: When I'm good and ready. Pretty soon.
BEN: I'm sure they'll all recognise your portrait.
SALLY: What? Of *you*. Are you joking? Who do
you think wants to recognise a portrait of *you*?
I should cut out on the hard stuff and just
tipple with your own spirits. Best for you. I've
better things to write about...
(*Pause.*)
BEN: Are you really going out with Raymond?
SALLY: Yes.
BEN: Right, well piss off then.
SALLY: I shall. I'm reading.

BEN: Reading. Writing books. Books. The world's a battlefield. No, a sewage farm of books. Look at them all. Written for people like you.

SALLY: And Glen.

BEN: At least they're good.

SALLY: A bubble. Of literary luminaries. Books about people who wrote books, painted pictures, made films – you said yourself we were choking ourselves to death with the effluent of celluloid.

BEN: I did. I try not to add to it.

SALLY: Don't worry. You will. As long as it gets flushed away...

(*Pause.*)

You'll have Shirley to comfort you and tell her how different she is from her sister.

BEN: She sure is.

SALLY: Will you tell her how much you despise her paltry middle-class Marxist daubings and her nanny-derived Maoist marches in Grosvenor Square and Hyde Park?

BEN: I already have. You remember quite well. She burst into tears in your room.

SALLY: The next time?

BEN: She laughed and said I was an old silly who didn't know what was going on.

SALLY: Bright girl!

BEN: Well, I told the truth. That's one thing I haven't learned to do with you.

(*Pause.*)

SALLY: I'm tired of this. Raymond!

(*RAYMOND comes in.*)

Let's take his Lordship's dog out for him. He'll never take her out himself and *he* wanted to film Francis of Assisi! Can you imagine: my little brothers and sisters!

RAYMOND: I'll get my wellies. It's wet.

SALLY: OK. I'll get mine. Fresh air's what we need.

(*They go to their respective rooms. BEN hesitates and then goes to the telephone, which he dials.*)

BEN: (*Phone.*) Hello. Chivers Hotel? May I speak
to Mrs Marion Silcox? Yes... Tell her it's Mr
Prosser. PROSSER. That's right...
(*Both SALLY and RAYMOND reappear, clad in macintosh
and wellingtons, dog's lead, etc.*)
(*As SALLY descends stairs.*)
Hello, Marion? Yes. It is... Ben. Look. I'm not
going, I say, I'm not going to talk for long... No,
I don't want to talk to her. I want to talk to you.
Will you come down? Yes, I know I said not. And
I don't want the child damaged. I say – I say we
can all be *over*-protected. Yes, if we don't watch it.
Yes. I know that's my fault. I wanted the minimum
of bloodshed... And, of, yes, of course, the result
was carnage all round. But as you said. Why
shouldn't we meet. We've been, well, years. Keep
the child in the hotel... Well, sort of separated...
You know what *she's* like. Everyone's like. Hanging
on, yes. What? No, please come... Oh, I don't
know. Any time when you can. I ask you – I'll be
here. I'm tired of being told *what* I want to do, *who*
I should see. Promise? Oh, it'll be ugly. What
else? What's left us that isn't ugly? Ring me when
you get here. It'll be alright.
(*SALLY snatches the phone from him as he struggles to keep
it away.*)
SALLY: Marion? Oh, yes, your strangled voice...
This is Sally. Yes, your ex-husband's wife. Do
come down if your runty little legs will stand.
Bring the brat. No-one will harm her. Certainly
not me. I wouldn't touch her. And, oh yes, fuck
him if you like. In my bed. I doubt if I shall be
here to watch the spectacle. But there will be
others. Goodbye...
(*She puts down the receiver and goes to the main door.*)
Got the lead, Raymond? We might take her in
the car for a bit.
(*She stands at the door. RAYMOND follows. Slowly, BEN
opens the gift box. He takes out the new outfit and*

unwrapping it slowly tears it into shreds. In front of them.
Systematically he throws them outside. Including the box.)
(*Presently.*) Time for walkies.

BEN: (*To RAYMOND.*) You wormy –

RAYMOND: Faggot?

SALLY: You shouldn't have thrown the box on the
rails. The line isn't yours yet you know!
(*They go out. BEN hurls some tissue paper after them and
closes the door. SHIRLEY watches from her door and comes
down. She gets him a drink and leads him to a sofa. Presently,
she kisses him.*)

BEN: You've always discouraged me before.

SHIRLEY: Events change. Time strikes... I'll leave
you. No, I'm *not* going to discuss Sally. That
doesn't mean I might not go to bed with you...
Now I think I'll go up and get the rest of the
light... I know what you think of me. But perhaps
you all think too much of personal relationships.
One, two, three, four...
(*She starts to go back to her room.*)
By the way, I'm not some malleable side of her
coin – or anyone else's.
(*She goes out, leaving him alone. In the other main room,
GLEN has awoken uneasily. JO goes to him.*)

JO: Darling.

GLEN: Jo. You're here.

JO: I'm here. How are you feeling?

GLEN: There was a lot of shouting. Noise. Voices.
In other rooms. All gone. All gone.

JO: Glen, you've not eaten again. Why won't you
see the doctor?

GLEN: Later. Later.

JO: Later. It's always later. You've finished
your book.

GLEN: Yes. Isn't it a relief. I think I feel hungry
enough for one of your dinners.

JO: I read it, well, the last of it, while you were
sleeping. My dear heart, I love you. I dread to
wake up and you not there.

GLEN: There are other voices. Other places. You
don't need mine.

JO: I do. I do. You are what I care for. The thing
that's left. Not fleeing away. I read your letters.
You are in my brain, not just my heart. Even in my
bed with others. I need your rebuke. Your smile
when I'm naughty or stupid and misunderstanding.
You've lit my silly schoolgirl life. You've brought
me up. Slapped life into me. Don't let me get old.
Not when you are still so young. I'm sorry. I can't
bear to be alone. For I *will* be. The rest means
so little, without you. My reading and silly
letters and walks with you and rides and my awful
home-weave cooking...

GLEN: Go and do some more.

JO: Tell me more. Your love, yes, the boys, the
desolation, even the *fame*. Keep your clothes
with mine here and your things. And my heart
in yours.

GLEN: It's there, my dearest. It *is* there. Always.

JO: Your spectacles. I've broken them...

GLEN: Ben and Sally have broken up.

JO: Yes. I know. Stay there. I'll be back.
(*She goes out, nodding at BEN.*)
Could I have a drink? I've just got to make a call.

BEN: Sure.
(*He gets one.*)

JO: Hello, Dr Ashton? Sorry to bother you, but yes;
I think he's getting worse. I know he should. But
perhaps if you come again? He's finished his
book... His... Well, anyway, if you could. When
you've time. No. Not *immediate*. 'Bye.

BEN: Worse?

JO: Yes.

BEN: How rotten.

JO: He seems better.

BEN: Which is a bad sign.

JO: Yes... I'm sorry about –

BEN: Oh, well. End of a long tunnel for all.

JO: I won't ask you any details. I must prepare the dinner.

BEN: I'll help you.

JO: How was your little girl?

BEN: Oh. It's nice to hear it *uninflected*. I don't know. What do I know about little girls? Or anyone, for that. Someone asked me once what I think of "young people" and I was more or less pilloried for it. How many or how much do *I* know. When I was a little boy, I didn't know much about other little boys. Except I didn't like them over much. Nor them me. Little girls, some yes, a lot.

JO: How was she?

BEN: Can I say this? Well, I will, on the way to, to: fierce, proud and gentle.

JO: Don't let them persuade you she doesn't love you. Even if she doesn't love you now – she, oh she will.

BEN: Hard to love a renegade father.

JO: You're not *my* renegade father. And *I* love you.

BEN: You love so many people.

JO: I know. You *suspect* it.

BEN: No. Like a believer, I *doubt*. You love Glen.

JO: Yes.

BEN: You can't think of life without him?

JO: No.

BEN: And me?

JO: Yes.

BEN: Why do you love me? I see why you love Glen.

JO: I love you because I *am* love for you. I am your child, your protector. Oh, doesn't it sound twee?

BEN: Yes. But TWUE.

JO: I am the seed in your earth. I shine on upon you and you are there always... Ben, perhaps not... (*Pause.*)

BEN: I was the, well the protagonist of the most degrading spectacle. Today.

157

JO: Tell me.

BEN: May I? There's no-one... I'll cut it right down.
I was sitting in the restaurant with my daughter.
She refused a cushion for her chair like she used
to have. Very politely. I looked at her. She looked
at me. I talked about the restaurant, the waiter,
the food, who went there, what dishes there were.
She ordered promptly, courteously. She tackled
her spaghetti, her steak, her ice-cream. Her coke.
We said less and less. I wanted her to go. *She*
wanted to go. To be with her friends, her mother,
I don't know who. I drank an extra half-litre of
wine. I ordered the wine. Got the bill in a hurry.
I looked at her, and, well, yes the awful, the thing
is I cried all over the tablecloth. In front of her.
She watched my jowls move. I looked away. But
I couldn't. Through the marble and columns and
the rest of the silencing restaurant and waiters
scrupulously *not* watching. I couldn't even get out
"Let's go". Then, suddenly, she leapt off her too
low chair and put her arms round me. And *she*
cried. Like a "B" movie. She took my hand and
we walked out past all the rows of tables. I left
her at home and we neither of us said a word;
just held hands; no, she knew the way home. Isn't
that despicable? How could I face her? That's
why I rang... I dare say...
(*Pause.*)

JO: We'll be such friends and lovers and not mind
being sentimental or even romantic if we
can manage.

BEN: We have been.

JO: What?

BEN: Friends and lovers.

JO: Yes. But we shall grow from a new childhood.
I shall crave for you and you'll quicken for me.
Even if there are others.

BEN: Does Glen know?

JO: Yes. He delights in it. It will be alright. That
of it as – *that!* It. Is. Now. Will be. Has been. We
are! We'll never really leave. Even if we get on
our nerves. Oh, Ben, I'm frightened! But I'm
alright. Kiss me... And later. All the rest and the
rest and the rest...
(*They embrace.*)
There's Glenny. Come in, my darling. We're so
happy suddenly, we've been kissing and cuddling
and your book's finished and we're going to have
roast lamb and peas from the garden and that
claret of yours. (*He is inside the room.*)

GLEN: Oh, my dear both.
(*He embraces them both. SHIRLEY enters.*)

SHIRLEY: (*Entering.*) Alright then.

JO: Shirley, Glen's finished his book. I love him.
I can't bear to go into his room. I love Ben, no,
you think I'm light-minded, a lot of people do.
Like they think about you. I think and welcome
you within all I know up to this now, this moment,
with my heart full and my brain clear and empty.
Forgive me for what I am not. But I am – I am
a loving creature... I'm frail and I break but bear
with me... It's hard to love, isn't it? It's like
religion without pain, I mean it's not religion
without pain. It's not flowers and light and
fellowship. It's cruel and we inhabit each other's
dark places. Let's drink to that. It's not much
worse than the rest. The time is short and all our
heads are sore and our hearts sick oh, into the
world, this century we've been born into and made
and been made by. Release us from ourselves and
give us each our other. There: I've said, I've
invented a grace, not very gracefully. Oh, Glen,
bless you, the life you've given me, at least, and
you Ben, for the work and pain you long to
exorcise, and you Shirley for being such a butt
with such human grace. Damn it, I didn't mean to
cry. How indecent.

BEN: It's been an indecent sort of day.

JO: Well, it won't be. We'll all have dinner and talk
and think of love, even if there are lumps of
hate within us. Please say yes. There isn't long.

GLEN: No. You're right. Say it while you can.
Naïvely, if you like. While you can. There will
be no counting, cant or otherwise. Cant on
Unchristian Soldiers.

SHIRLEY: Are we drunk already?

GLEN: No. And what would it matter. I have...
tried to love. No, I *have* loved. I love Jo.
I love you (*To BEN.*) and the rest of you.

SHIRLEY: We *are* drunk already.

BEN: No. We're not! We *will* be but we're not. It's
too late to persist in our folly.

GLEN: Or to become wise.

BEN: Oh, come, you're wise. You're very wise.

GLEN: No I'm not. I took to writing about people
in recent times because I thought it might show
us what we are yesterday and today. They're
starting to wonder. But too late. My book's no
good. It's too late. The century pulled the carpet
out from me. Cleverness and all.

BEN: My films are not much. What does it matter?
Her paintings are no good and her protests are
a terribly real joke on us all. Her (Jo's) love is no
good. How can you be a romantic in a world that
despises imagination and only gives instruction in
orgasms? The response and admiration of virtues.
Where? Now. It's not in the crushing of the worm
of will. The imagination.

GLEN: The cast worm forgives the plough.

BEN: Oh, shut up, my dead darling.

GLEN: Strive, no, arrive at detachment.

BEN: I wish I had. Strive for apathy. Hope and
fear. Members of one another.

JO: We're a rag bag. A glorious, silly old rag bag!

BEN: Providence, duty, the sufficiency of virtue.

SHIRLEY: You *are* stoned.

BEN: No. Noiseless terror.

GLEN: English Catholicism was different, but it saw that the whole future was to be decided by the sheer amount of its noise.

SHIRLEY: Anyone hungry yet?

BEN: What will it be *like*? It hasn't begun to *work*. Us. The twentieth century. You (*To SHIRLEY.*) hate us. Why do they hate us? They'll be worse off. More frightened, more huddling for comfort. They do it now. Thin and careless like none of us has ever been. Precept: be bold. There will never be more perfection than there is now. Glen and Jo are together. Shall we lie in bed?

SHIRLEY: No.

BEN: Quite right. Improper. Suggestion. Anyway, I lust for Jo. What *will* it be like? Time future. Now, this is, this is saloon bar. Bar talk. Do you know the worst cut they made on the road?

GLEN: I can think of several.

BEN: My God, my God, why has Thou forsaken me?

GLEN: Not bad.

SHIRLEY: My God – you sicken me.

BEN: Good. That was my patent intention.

GLEN: I *did* always delight in the Absurd. But where is it *gone*?

BEN: Bullies. Bullies who tell you what to do and think. Like Shirley. Do you know the Edwardians must have been the last to have known that *their* appearance – at the expense of others, mark, gave pleasure to others.

GLEN: I was the last of them, about.

BEN: Age cant. Past. Present. Futurology. Now, how do you get to be a futurologist?

JO: Take a Master's degree.

BEN: The way it *will* be. Is. Not long to go. Glenny, my darling, end-of-term one. Kiss me. (*They embrace.*)

May I kiss Jo?
(*He does so. Passionately.*
GLEN watches in a, yes, exquisite desolation.)
Ah, the old, silent life of England, eh Shirley?
SHIRLEY: And good riddance.
BEN: You do alright out of the residue of it. Seeing
     revolutionary worlds in a grain of sand, eh,
     chucky, chucky.
GLEN: *I* never liked the judicial tone...
BEN: Oh, it will totter on. Glen will write about
     the twentieth century and the people who lived
     it. Shirley will paint and barricade. Jo will take
     lovers. I will grow old in films... Oh God... this
     is a loveless place.
     (*The main door opens. SALLY and RAYMOND appear. She
     is carrying the dead wet body of a largish dog. She moves into
     the room. Presently.*)
SALLY: They shot her. She was on heat and we
     stupidly let her fly off miles away. We saw them
     from the top of the hill, helpless. They tied, yes
     tied her to a tree and set all the male dogs on
     her. And then they shot her... In front of us.
SHIRLEY: Oh God.
SALLY: Pigs, all of you. Why don't you ring the vet?
RAYMOND: She's dead, darling.
SALLY: Here she is. *Your.* Your dog.
     (*She staggers upstairs. RAYMOND takes the animal's body
     from BEN.*)
RAYMOND: I'll take her.
     (*BEN rushes after her, up the stairs. She turns.*)
SALLY: *Your* dog!
     (*He goes to put an arm round her. She hits him in the face.
     He staggers, recovers and they begin hitting each other. The
     rail breaks and she falls to the ground.*)
     You've broken my back!
BEN: Good!
     (*He jumps down. Almost on top of her.*)
     It was *my* dog. And *you've* broken *my* back.

SALLY: Do something, someone. Let
something *happen*!
BEN: Keep away. I'll kill her! I'll kill her! She's
killed *me*. She's killed *everything*. Long ago.
SALLY: I haven't. But I would. And somebody will!
(*He smashes her in the face, and they kick and tear at each
other, clothes tearing and splitting. Blood and breakage. The
others watch them fight while RAYMOND holds the dead dog
in his arms.*)
(*Curtain.*)

ACT TWO

The following day. Same set. JO is sitting alone in the main set.
GLEN is lying in his room, watched over by BEN. SALLY comes
down the stairs.

JO: I've made some tea. Good British custom after
the blitz.

SALLY: Is the doctor here yet?

JO: No. Don't fret.

SALLY: I am.

JO: Of course.

SALLY: You think he's dying?

JO: Of course. For ages. What's left? Now?

SALLY: Indeed. I think my jaw's broken.

JO: Oh, my dear.

SALLY: I don't think it matters much. Do you?
What isn't broken? Dead? Disappearing?

JO: Oh, Sally. Don't.

SALLY: What?

JO: Split up.

SALLY: That doesn't seem to matter much either. It's
there. But it's gone. Another horseless carriage.

JO: I love you both.

SALLY: You love Ben?

JO: Yes.

SALLY: And Glen?

JO: Glen is the life. If he goes. It all. Goes. Gone.
The wit, the irony, the kindness, the struggle
with himself which he never unburdened.

SALLY: No. He didn't do that...

JO: He was a *friend,* Sally. A man of friendship. He
clove to your silliness and never betrayed you.
People said he was a bitch but he wasn't.

SALLY: Isn't.

JO: He had high standards but he kept them for
himself. He didn't admire what he was, which
was a great deal, but admired a lot of the others.

I broke his spectacles... I can't bear the room without him. His forehead. His breathing. His arcane jokes and odd fancies. I love his old clothes. His letters and his bad drawings. His restless indolence. His sickly athleticism. His tolerance and forbearing. Oh, I'm going on as if he's dead. But he's breathing heavily in my heart, more than he ever did. Oh, Glen, my brilliant, kindly, silly Glen. You listened to my chirruping and ate my home-made jam which you didn't like. Your frail, fastidious, greedy body, loving, full of lust and circumspection... He was ashamed of his boys, you know. No, not ashamed of them but himself, his own odd body and over-turning mind. He would listen to my affairs with men, my daft letters and exchange drawings, make jokes I didn't understand and didn't mind. He loved me, he *did,* didn't he?

SALLY: He did. The best of a poor world for you both... Do you love me?

JO: Yes. I always have.

SALLY: Like you love Ben?

JO: Oh, same only different. You know...

SALLY: Because I've got to love you. Gotten, as the Americans say. You rouse my inside with – with – your caprice, your enthusiasm, your odd, withdrawn moods. Your strong, thriving body, your sturdy legs and hard arms, I –

JO: Yes?

SALLY: No. Glen's in your being now.

JO: You can't drive that out.

SALLY: No.

JO: Do you want to make love to me?

SALLY: Yes. I want to kiss you. On the mouth. My tongue between your bright teeth. I want to hold you in my arms a whole night with our bodies like twin fortresses, lap in lap. I want to see you wake up and look down at me and get me awake... May I kiss you?

JO: As long as you want. *I* want you to. (*They kiss, gently, forcibly.*)

SALLY: They'd call us a couple of old diesels.

JO: Who cares? Glen wouldn't.

SALLY: Jo... Let's go away. When it's all over. And you think you can and still want to. I know it's not the time but, yes, it *is* the time. Because it's running out, and we should be running away, running away together where we see fit or fine... I really do love you. *I'm tired of the bodies of men.* They've gone through my life and I'm just like a, oh, closed line, service discontinued. We could go on for as long as we like. Oh, Jo, I want to hold you and cuddle you and rest in your body...

JO: My darling. (*They kiss again.*)

SALLY: Oh, your body. The next few weeks, months will be foul. But be patient. I've tried to learn. Give us a chance. No-one else will. We'll dress in what we want, go where we like, think of each other as well as the rest. You are so – near. Dear. Don't let this chance slide. It won't occur again. Other lines aren't the same.

JO: What about Ben?

SALLY: Ben thinks he needs me. *I* thought so. But he'll be so *relieved*. Especially if it's you and me. He might even make a film out of it. Promise! Say promise! No. Don't *say*. Just nod...
(*JO nods. They embrace.*)

JO: People laugh at this sort of thing. Like poor Glen.

SALLY: (*Mad!*) Well, Ben wouldn't do that.

JO: Is Ben –

SALLY: Oh, I've stupidly told him he is. And he's always wandering – naturally. But I don't think so. He's a wanderer. Stay at home nomad, rather.

JO: Sally?

SALLY: Jo...

JO: Sally...

SALLY: Jo. Oh, Jo, joke, Sally of *OUR* alley. I love you in a hundred ways and I won't look up one

anthology to tell you how. Strange. I wanted to love my sister. But I didn't. Ben wanted to love his sister – like an extra wife to carry the burden. But she died. And left him with me. Oh, and Marion. His father. His mother. And his daughter. Thank heavens *we'll* have no children, Jo. Jo and Sally – our own offspring. Hold me again. No man's held me like that since I can't remember. (*Doorbell rings.*)
Now let's wipe our eyes. That'll be the doctor. It'll be hard, Jo. But don't forget this when you're going through it all. It'll still be there when it's time. Glen would like it.

JO: Shall I tell him?

SALLY: Up to you.
(*SALLY goes to the front door and ushers in DR ASHTON.*)
Good morning, Dr Ashton. Thanks for coming so soon.

ASHTON: Nasty cut and bruise on your face. Alright, are you?

SALLY: Oh yes, rural life. You know.

ASHTON: How's the patient?

SALLY: You *said* it. Worse.

ASHTON: I'm not surprised. I told Miss – er – here months ago. Hospital was the place.

SALLY: Not a railway station.

ASHTON: This is the way, isn't it? Booking hall?

JO: Shall I come?

ASHTON: If you wish. Perhaps not.
(*She follows him into the room. BEN goes out. She follows him as the DOCTOR examines him. SALLY goes upstairs, leaving BEN and JO alone. He grasps her hand, which she takes uncertainly.*)

BEN: Alright?

JO: No... Scared.

BEN: Don't be. Sally?

JO: She's fine. She says you've broken her jaw.

BEN: I couldn't break a sparrow's jaw.
(*Pause.*)
Jo, I do love you.

JO: I know.

BEN: And you?

JO: Yes.

BEN: We could sift something out of the rubble. I want to hold you. Now, I'm afraid.

JO: I know. So do I. But Glen's dying in there. That's where I should be now.

(She goes into GLEN's room. The DOCTOR is already leaving and moves to the main set.)

ASHTON: I don't like to move him but I'll get him into the cottage hospital straight away. It's early *(Looks at watch.)* – as soon as I can.

JO: Cottage hospital! Can't you get him to London?

ASHTON: I doubt if he'd make it. Sorry. I'll be back. Soon as I can.

SALLY: Dr Ashton – is it –

ASHTON: Yes. I'm afraid it is. Very soon. I'll find my way across the platform. I'm sorry.

(He goes. JO lets out a great howl and hurls herself into the other room on to GLEN's still figure. Pause.)

BEN: Oh, well.

SALLY: Well, what?

(RAYMOND and SHIRLEY have appeared.)

BEN: It's Glen. Er, Jo. He's for the chopper. Right away.

SALLY: Right away? Well, what?

BEN: Well, we all have to go sometime, as my old mother used to say.

SALLY: I wish *she'd* go! Have you taken her cupper tea up to her yet? Well, I will. And I'll smash her face in with it. Like you did mine. See what you did.

BEN: Beautiful bone structure unaltered.

SALLY: If you were a man –

BEN: I've never claimed so much. Perhaps *you* should. Your uppercut's better than mine. *And* your feet and knees.

SALLY: If you had any balls, I'd have kicked them into the siding.

BEN: Still British Railways property. Till the end of the month. Alright are we all then?

SALLY: I'm going for a walk. Jo, come for a walk. Ben'll stay – if he can.

BEN: Yes. I will.

(*JO appears at the door.*)

JO: He did love me. His eyes are so blue – and he held my hand so tight it hurt.

SALLY: Come for a walk.

JO: No. I'll wait. On the platform. The sun's up now. It's warm.

(*SALLY clasps her. She closes the door.*)

SALLY: Right. Walkies. Till the doc returns.

RAYMOND: I think I'll stay in case I'm needed.

SALLY: OK. Shirley?

SHIRLEY: Right. Bit of exercise.

BEN: Bit of exercise!

SALLY: Shut up, you!

BEN: And you shut up, fat-mouth. A friend's dying in there.

SALLY: No friend of yours. Come on, Shirley. (*To JO.*) Raymond will get you anything you want. Gormless won't.

JO: Thanks. I'll just wait.

(*SALLY and SHIRLEY go out.*)

SALLY: Wish *I* had a shotgun today.

(*Exit.*)

JO: I'll just sit outside I think. It's quite warm.

(*BEN embraces her.*)

BEN: Just wait. It's ridiculous to say it. But wait. Get drunk. Sleep. It will pass. I want you... I shouldn't have said that.

JO: Why not? If you mean it. Glen would be pleased. Oh, Glen.

BEN: There...

JO: Glen come back. I can't live – with all this. Who can? *You* couldn't even. Do we give up...

(*She disengages herself from BEN.*)

Sorry. I'll sit in the sun till the doctor comes back.

BEN: Be careful.

JO: Of what?

BEN: Oh, pedestrian traffic.

(He sits alone after she's gone out. RAYMOND comes in from the kitchen.)

RAYMOND: Thought I'd bury the dog while they're all out.

BEN: Thoughtful.

RAYMOND: Do you want anything? Coffee?

BEN: No thanks, Raymond. I've got some on.

RAYMOND: Well, I think I'll look in on him. While I have my coffee. They're all out. Except Mum. Why don't you get some sleep?

BEN: Right. Thanks.

RAYMOND: I'll look out for the doctor. Where's Jo?

BEN: Outside. In the platform sun.

RAYMOND: See you then.

BEN: See you.

(RAYMOND goes.)

I hope not. Oh...

(He settles into the sofa. In the other room, RAYMOND hovers over GLEN.)

RAYMOND: Glen?

GLEN: Ah... Raymond. What is it you've got to tell me? Doctor not here, I hope. Hope he's too late again, that one.

RAYMOND: Can I –

GLEN: I can hear you, you –

RAYMOND: Faggot.

GLEN: Faggots were not so long ago what the working classes used to eat. With peas, I think. And saveloys.

RAYMOND: How would you know?

GLEN: Guardsman told me.

RAYMOND: You bet.

GLEN: Tell me something. If you will.

RAYMOND: What?

GLEN: Were they really separating? Sally and Ben?

RAYMOND: No. Least, not at the time. It was like they wanted you all to decide for them.

GLEN: What a disgusting notion. Whose idea was it?

RAYMOND: Hers, I think, but he went along with it in the end. Didn't know what they were doing, either of them.

GLEN: Quite. But to use your friends and *test* them – it's like vivisection on friendship.

RAYMOND: Depends how you feel. I don't think she went much on you.

GLEN: I know. But I admired her. Made more, far more than there was of herself. Well, thanks for telling me. Try not to tell the others. If you can. Especially Jo.

RAYMOND: Well, it's all over bar the shouting, isn't it? I don't mean you, with, well, respect. But what's left in it for any of us?

GLEN: Well, if this is terminal care I can't say I think much of it.

RAYMOND: Doctor'll be here soon.

GLEN: To hell with the doctor. Where's Jo?

RAYMOND: Sunning herself on the platform with the weighing machines. She's alright. I'll wait here till she comes back. Right?

GLEN: Just as you like... I saw two signs on the road coming down. One was a little triangle of green with a hedge and a bench. And a sign read: "This is a temporary open space..."

RAYMOND: Oh yes?

GLEN: And the other was a site of rubble near the Crystal Palace I think, perched high up over London, where the bank managers and cashiers fled at the beginning of our – our – of our century. It said 'Blenkinsop – Demolitionists. We *do* it. You *watch* it. *Come down.*'

(*He recedes from consciousness and RAYMOND reads a magazine with his coffee at the bedside. The door of the main set opens and MARION enters. She is expensively dressed in a tight-fitting fur coat. Slightly younger than BEN.*)

171

MARION: Darling!

BEN: Marion!

MARION: Ben!

(*They embrace.*)

Are you all alone?

BEN: Sally and Shirley have gone for a walk. The dog's died.

MARION: Oh, darling, you loved that dog.

BEN: Yes, but nobody believed it. Like they don't believe I love our child. Anyone.

MARION: I do. And she does.

BEN: Raymond is in the next room watching over poor darling old Glen – dying fast.

MARION: God!

BEN: And Jo is ice-cold in the morning sun outside.

MARION: That must have been the girl I saw on the platform. Like, well, rather like Sally.

BEN: That's the one.

MARION: The one you wanted to have because –

BEN: They were sisters? That was someone else. Marion. That's nothing at all. Why has it got all so bad, so brutish, so devilish, so sneering?

MARION: Calm down, darling. Shall I get you some coffee? Or a drink at this good, early hour.

BEN: Oh, your voice is so *easy*. Just hold on to me. And talk. First: information.

MARION: Well, at first I was utterly bewildered. I *knew* you'd had a bad time with the offspring. Though she didn't say a word. She loves you.

BEN: Why? What for.

MARION: She's yours. She likes you. She admires you.

BEN: For what? Being a renegade father's no great shakes. You, know, you know Sally's made me sound like a Hollywood movie. Me! I turned down three million, no five plus a percentage, dollars not to. I'm English I said – what's that any more – I *live* here and I don't want your filthy dollars and broken impulses... You look rather lovely at this time of the day.

MARION: I don't. And neither do you. But I can see why. Anyway, when Sally hawked her usual bile down the phone, I wasn't sure what to do. I wasn't going to bring our fledgling, in spite of what you said. Broken noses and obscenities are just about enough for you and me. But, no, I left *her* at the hotel with the nanny. But I *had* to see you. And I don't care about the broken bottles and flick knives. It's all violent and we've got to find a way out of it. I'm so sorry about Glen. Is it?

BEN: Yes. Any old time I'd say. Raymond or Jo or Sally will keep us informed.

MARION: He loved you, Ben.

BEN: Did he, Marion? I don't know anything about all of that any more. I think he loved me once. I loved him. Oh, I did. They all thought *I* was a pouf. But I loved him. I loved him because, because he was him and he made his own life out of the twentieth century and what a bad one *it* was. The century, I mean. But he didn't trim, he didn't deceive himself, he preened his perverse English personality and grinned at everyone, and made them feel better, things more likely to happen but not matter anyway. He loved and was loved. And in spite of fearing both of it. I am neither loved nor loving... Except I want *you* at this moment.

MARION: Ben, let's go. I've the car outside. We *can* do it.

BEN: Maybe we can. But not now. I can't leave Glen. To that bleeding Raymond. And Sally and Shirley. Jo, well she's different.

MARION: *You* love her?

BEN: In a way. She's a loving thing from an unknown attic. Take your clothes off. I want you.

MARION: Certainly not. I want *you*. But I do have to drive back. And I don't really fancy being caught by Jackboots Sally.

173

BEN: I shouldn't have said that to you.

MARION: You shouldn't have said a lot of things.
Did you tell her we went to bed yesterday?

BEN: She assumed it, anyway. So, I, I reserved my
position. Fat lot of good it did too. Nearly got
killed. She's so *strong*. And I'm out well, well
out of condition.

MARION: Ben, I know you. Do believe me. You
wake up. You know how. Not "about" anything.
It's just black and fearsome and impossible to
get up. Sweat and loathing. All too early. You
can't read or concentrate or remember. You sleep
endlessly between good or bad times. It's all the
same. We've become islands at the edges of the
bed. You're on your own. I'm on *my* own. Now,
for years. Oh, Ben, it's been a glass steel wall.
Both observing the child and her us. We do –
did nothing with her – or her with us. I tried
keeping her out of the bedroom, for my sake as
much as yours. We never did things at the same
time of day. We couldn't. I followed you like
a dog when I knew you wanted to be left alone.
You wanted to sleep in front of the television.

BEN: I know: it's true. You read about it in the
papers: "A Wife's Problems." "How I won
through. Why did he want so desperately to be
alone!" Stupid nit. We did love each other.
Dearly. But it was all risk, risk, damned risk,
gambling. Russian roulette.

MARION: We had our moments, oh, who cares,
our moments of happiness? Months of
happiness. Penniless and odd but relaxing,
forgetful happiness.

BEN: We did. You helped. We helped. You see: the
more pain I FEEL, the more resentment comes
out of *her*.

MARION: Come back, Ben. Do, do come, Ben. I'll
tell you everything that's happened and you can

tell me everything that's happened. And we'll go through what's happened with us. It wasn't half bad...

BEN: No. It wasn't...

MARION: We should have trusted each other then. Instead of going our ways. Blindly. Hoping. You can't *hope* any longer. Oh, Ben, come *now*. Before they all come back and *she* starts smashing the place up. And *I* get scared and run. And you give up... Let's go now. Give ourselves a chance. Glen wouldn't mind... Neither would Jo.

BEN: Give me time, Marion. Darling.

MARION: There's been a lot of time. A wasteland of it. For all of us. I think I'll go for a walk and then I'll get into the car and drive back to London. It's in the old car park. With a couple of others. I'll wait half an hour.

(*As she gets up to go, SALLY and SHIRLEY appear at the door.*)

I'm sorry to be so early. I'm just going.

(*SALLY says nothing. Nor SHIRLEY. BEN sees her out uneasily.*)

SALLY: Well, did you fuck her?

BEN: Oh, shut up, pig mouth. He's *dying* in there.

SALLY: Were you waiting till he was cold?

BEN: What else do you think of?

SALLY: Plenty. How's Glen?

BEN: Ask Raymond.

SALLY: Raymond! How's Glen?

(*RAYMOND appears.*)

RAYMOND: I think – he's dead.

BEN: You *think*.

SALLY: What will *you* think.

(*BEN lurches into the other room. He examines the body fairly curiously while the others wait. He reappears.*)

BEN: Cottage hospital. Come on!

SALLY: I don't know why people make such a fuss about death. They do it all *for* you.

BEN: For you, maybe. Because you don't
know anything.

SALLY: Yes?

BEN: Yes. You'd better be an ignorant Negro in
Harlem spending a fortune.

SALLY: Oh, spare me. Promise me, if, no, when I die
this year probably, a good year for me, lay me in
the cold, cold ground of the smartest, sharpest,
nearest, fastest furnace burning they've got.

BEN: (*To RAYMOND.*) Did you tell him about Sally
and me?

RAYMOND: What?

BEN: What! That the whole thing was a shoddy
hoax from the start. Even if it looked true to all
of us, to Sally and me, it was disgusting and
a hoax and an insult and a wound to everyone.

SALLY: Piety again. *You* agreed to it.

BEN: Then I was wrong. Bloody, damn wrong.

RAYMOND: He'd guessed already.

BEN: But you didn't disabuse him?

RAYMOND: What?

BEN: You didn't let him die better in not knowing
the truth?

SALLY: Why shouldn't he know the truth. Just
because he was dying? Best time to find
out. Smoke out the prig, Raymond. It won't
be difficult.

BEN: I'll get Jo.

SALLY: Why don't you? The field's open.

RAYMOND: Anything for anyone?

SALLY: Yes. Let's have something good – fine but
robust for Glen's departure. Is there any
chocolate cake?

RAYMOND: As always.

SALLY: Right. Chocolate cake and champagne. See
the old thing off well before the doctor gets
here. OK Shirley?

SHIRLEY: I love chocolate cake. Especially for
breakfast. *And* champagne.

RAYMOND: Right.

(*BEN returns.*)

BEN: She won't come in. At least, till the doctor and the ambulance come.

SALLY: Probably right... I thought old Glen did rather well. He spent all his young years pretending to be older and all his older ones pretending to be younger. Now, *that's* a difficult feat.

BEN: I don't think you really –

SALLY: What? Yes.

BEN: Have feelings for anyone. Except dogs.

SALLY: *Your* dog.

BEN: My dog... How *little* you know.

SALLY: How little *you* know.

SHIRLEY: Oh, don't.

(*There is the faint huff and hoot of a small goods train on the line outside.*)

SALLY: Ah, the weekly goods that upsets Ben so much.

SHIRLEY: Early.

RAYMOND: No. Dead on time. What *can* they be shifting!

SALLY: Coffins!

RAYMOND: Jo's the only one –

(*They listen as the train moves through the station. Then it screeches to a stop. BEN runs out. They all wait. BEN returns with the body of JO in his arms.*)

BEN: She knew the time alright. I'll put her with Glen.

(*He carries her into the other room, followed by RAYMOND.*)

SALLY: I think we'll have coffee and, some will still want old English Breakfast. Hey?

(*DOCTOR ASHTON arrives at the open door.*)

ASHTON: She seems to have thrown herself right in front of the goods train. It was going slowly, but even so...

SALLY: Even so...

ASHTON: I've got the ambulance for Mr –

SALLY: Dear Glen. How difficult life will start to
become when he and his kind, with their villas
in Florence, their grasp of all things Greek
disappears. Oh, and their New York apartments
and erudition and all that, all that disappears,
don't you think, Dr Ashton?

ASHTON: I didn't really know much about him.
He wasn't really a patient of mine.

SALLY: But you *must* have known of him. Everyone
knew Glen from Berenson down to Maugham via
Cunard Junction.

ASHTON: Really?

SALLY: Really, Dr Ashton. You must tear yourself
away from the *Lancet* some time. You'll get
a very wealthy type of customer.
(*There's the sound of shooting from the railway. Glass starts
to break and it is soon clear that the place is being shot up.
Windows smash and things break up.*)

ASHTON: I'd better ring the police. Yobbos, I'm
afraid. You, you're not popular.

SALLY: How awful to be popular.

ASHTON: Then I'd better see the patient.

SALLY: Too late, alas. Dadie Rylands, this is your
life! Again.
(*BEN comes out of GLEN's room in an incoherent rage,
shouting and rushes out on to the platform.*)

ASHTON: (*On phone.*) Sergeant. Oh, sorry. Trouble
at the old railway halt. That's the one. Don't
know, sort of yobbos, I think. Anyway, they're
smashing up the place. And I have two patients
for the cottage hospital and – yes. Soon as
you can...
(*BEN reappears, all shot up.*)

BEN: They – shot – at – the – body.

ASHTON: Yes. Two. Maybe three. Or more.
(*He examines the body of the dead JO while the station is shot
to pieces around them.*)

Get everyone together. In the safest place...
You've brought this on yourselves, you know.

SALLY: I dare say. If it's any comfort to you.

ASHTON: Number Three by all accounts.

BEN: RAYMOND! RAYMOND! Come and look after your Sally.

(*RAYMOND appears.*)

ASHTON: Here, give me a hand.

(*RAYMOND approaches.*)

BEN: Look after her, Raymond. I know I can rely on you... even when I'm *bleeding* to death.

SALLY: Oh, Ben, don't go. Don't leave me. We all, *the few of us,* need one another.

(*BEN is clearly almost dead or in a coma.*)

ASHTON: Well, you do lead odd sorts of lives, don't you.

(*The station is fast becoming a wreck and the police sirens are sounding.*)

SALLY: Yes. We do, Dr Ashton. We do. Most of us. You must be glad.

(*Curtain.*)

The End.

Also published by Oberon Books:

John Osborne *The Picture of Dorian Gray*
ISBN: 1 84002 103 9

John Osborne *Four Plays:*
The End of Me Old Cigar
A Sense of Detchment
A Place Calling Itself Rome
Jill and Jack
ISBN: 1 84002 074 1